The POWER OF A STORY

It

INSPIRES,
SURPRISES
AND LIFTS

YOUR FAITH

JAMES W. MOORE

Abing
Na

THE POWER OF A STORY

Copyright 2014 © by Abingdon Press

Library of Congress Cataloging-in-Publication Data has been requested.

ISBN 978-1-4267-8774-4

14 15 16 17 18 19 20 21 22 23—10 9 8 7 6 5 4 3 2 1

MANUFACTURED IN THE UNITED STATES OF AMERICA

For our grandchildren,

Sarah, Paul, Dawson, Daniel, and Mason.

We call them "grand" because they are!

CONTENTS

Contents

Contents

INTRODUCTION:
THE POWER OF A STORY

I first noticed it as a little boy sitting in church beside my grandmother with my feet dangling off the front of the pew: I loved a good story!

I would be sitting there in the sanctuary of our church doing what young boys do in church—drawing pictures on the back of the bulletin, working puzzles, looking constantly at Granny's watch wishing the second hand would move faster, daydreaming about sports, kicking my feet in the air impatiently, counting the organ pipes—and then, the minister would start telling a story and I was hooked! The preacher had my full attention. I couldn't wait to hear the story!

I especially liked stories that made a good point, stories that challenged you to think, stories that taught a key lesson about life, stories that prompted you to laugh, stories that had a surprise ending, stories that inspired you to do better and be better, stories that underscored and clarified the amazing truths of the Christian faith.

And, would you believe it? Even though many years have passed since those golden days at St. Mark's Church in Memphis, Tennessee, I haven't changed at all with regard to my love for stories. I still love good stories— stories that teach, stories that preach, stories that touch your heart and stretch your mind.

For that reason, I have always included lots of stories in my sermons and in my books. I think it is one of the very best ways to reach people with the good news of the gospel.

Look at the Bible! It is filled with incredible stories, stories that have been treasured by people all over the globe for thousands of years, stories that have taught us life's most valuable lessons.

And look at Jesus! He loved stories and so often used them to convey his message and to capture the hearts of his listeners. His parables are, without question, some of the greatest stories ever told. And they are timeless, as relevant today as on the day he told them.

So, with all of that in mind, that's what this book is all about. Here you will find a variety of stories that will highlight important and valuable lessons about faith, hope, and love, but even more (hopefully and prayerfully) they will move us to a deeper love for God and a deeper love for other people.

Do you remember Jesus's response when he was asked what the greatest commandment is? He said it is to love God and love your neighbor. Then when the questioner pressed the issue by asking, "Yes, but who is my neighbor?" what did Jesus do? He told one of the best stories of all, the parable of the good Samaritan. In doing that, once again, he showed us dramatically, The Power of a Story!

FINDING GOD IN UNEXPECTED PLACES

Have you ever met God in an unexpected place? Some of the most memorable moments in the scriptures are those stories of people running into God in surprising, unexpected places.

Moses, in exile in the wilderness, experienced God in a burning bush.

Jacob, in the most fearful moment of his life—wrestling with his soul—found God there.

Job, grappling with tragedy, sorrow, heartache, and physical pain, found God there.

Paul, on the Damascus Road in the midst of a vigilante hunt to find and destroy Christians, encountered God there.

Zacchaeus, while perched up in a sycamore tree, the picture of loneliness and rejection, met God there.

Shadrach, Meshach, and Abednego found him in a fiery furnace.

Daniel found him in a lion's den.

And in the Gospels, look where people find him: with shepherds in a field, with fishermen by the sea, in sickness, in hunger, in sadness, in failure, in the Garden of Gethsemane, and on a hill faraway called Golgotha.

A few years ago, some close friends of ours in Tennessee suddenly and tragically lost their youngest daughter.

Her name was Ellen. She was sitting in the den of their home one Sunday evening, laughing and talking with her mother. Suddenly, with no warning, her leg went numb and then her arm. Then she fell back paralyzed and unconscious. So quickly it had happened.

She was rushed to the hospital where brain surgery was performed. The operation lasted all night. She died the next morning—sixteen years old!

When I received the heart-wrenching news of her death, I called to express my love, to try to minister to these dear friends. Instead, they ministered to me. Ellen's mother said, "God is giving us strength we didn't know we could have. He is seeing us through this. He keeps reminding us that we got to have Ellen for sixteen years and that she packed more life and love into sixteen years than most people do in a lifetime. We are all right. Don't worry about us because God is with us as never before!"

"God is with us as never before," she said. They had found God many, many times before in expected places—in church, in the scriptures, in prayer, at the altar, in joys and blessings and good times—but now he was there with them as never before in the unexpected place of tragedy and sorrow.

The Apostle Paul, writing to the church at Rome, put it beautifully as he said, "If God is for us, who is against us? . . . Who will separate us from the love of Christ? Will hardship, or distress, or persecution, or famine, or nakedness, or peril, or sword? . . . No, in all these things we are more than conquerors through him who loved us. . . . [Nothing] in all creation will be able to separate us from the love of God in Christ Jesus our Lord" (Romans 8:31-39).

ARE YOU STANDING IN GOD'S WAY?

Recently a man stopped by my office to see me. After we had visited about the weather and other such things, suddenly his face turned very serious and he said, "Jim, I have something I must talk with you about. I have been standing in God's way for sixteen years now and at this moment I'm having to live with the consequences of that." He paused for a moment and then continued, "It's my daughter. She is sixteen now and seems to always be in trouble—just one thing after another. She needs the church so very much but she has quit it altogether. She won't have anything to do with the church, and I feel it is my fault. I have been trying to get her to come back, but she only says, 'Who are you to talk to me about the church? You never encouraged me before and your church record surely isn't anything to shout about.' And what hurts," he said, "is that she is probably right."

"You see, Jim," he said, "I'm someone who wouldn't live in a community that didn't have a good church but I've always been willing to let somebody else see to it. It's so easy to sleep in on Sunday morning or go to the lake or just be lazy around the house. It's so easy to be light about religion or make jokes about the church. I'm not a bad guy. I've really tried to be a good father. I've given my daughter everything, trips to Europe, the best clothes, a car, the country club, a generous weekly allowance. I've given her everything, everything, that is, except what really counts. I have failed her in what matters most. She has seen in me a lack of commitment to God and his church."

He went on to say, "By my lack of dedication, by my cynical attitude, by my spiritual laziness, I have accidentally and tragically taught my daughter that God and the church are not important to me. Now I realize that for sixteen years I have been standing in God's way."

Now, this man's experience puts before us a probing question, namely, What about us? Are we standing in God's way? The question for us today is, How do we measure up? Does our influence really come down on God's side? Or are we a hindrance to God?

In the small-group movement that is so popular today, an interesting word has come into common usage to describe someone who hinders the group. It is called *blocking*. Blocking is anything that stops or slows down the group process. I just wonder if you or I ever block the kingdom of God. I wonder if we slow it down or impede its progress. Think about that for just a minute. Really, now, how do you measure up? What do other people do because of you?

Do people sense the importance of the church because of you?

Do people want to commit their lives to God because of you?

Do people want to be good and kind and loving because of you?

If not, you may be blocking God. You may be standing in God's way. You know, you don't have to be a dramatic, rebellious, prolific sinner to be a hindrance to God and his kingdom.

When William Temple, the famous Archbishop of Canterbury, was a student at Oxford, he went one day to hear a noted American evangelist. The evangelist preached long and hard on the forgiveness of God. Over and over the preacher quoted the text, "Though your sins be as scarlet, they shall be as white as snow."

Afterward, William Temple said, "Though I went to the meeting in a serious, inquiring spirit, I found myself quite unmoved, for alas, my sins were not scarlet, they

were gray—all gray. They were not dramatic acts of re-
belliousness or violent self-affirmation, but the colorless,
tired sins of omission, inertia, and timidity."

It's the little "gray" sins that may get in God's way
most of all and cause the most damage.

Surely, Jesus realized this. Maybe this is why he rebuked Simon Peter so firmly at Caesarea Philippi. Remember what happened there?

At Caesarea Philippi, Jesus announced to his disciples
that he was determined to go on to Jerusalem where he
would face great difficulties, but where he must go to
do the work he was committed to do. You remember
Simon Peter tried to block him, he tried to stop him, he
tried to talk him out of going. Then, according to the
Scriptures, Jesus turned and said those dramatic words
to Peter, "Get behind me, Satan! You are a stumbling
block to me; for you are setting your mind not on divine
things but on human things" (Matthew 16:23). This is a
very significant passage of scripture. They are haunting
words because they prompt us to ask ourselves some
very probing questions: What about me? Am I blocking
the coming of his Kingdom? Do I get in God's way?

"Get behind me, Satan! You are a stumbling block to
me." I just wonder how many times God has wanted to
say that to me. I mean well, but so did Simon Peter. Am
I, are you, standing in God's way?

THE SIN OF
PRESUMPTUOUS RELIGION

To be presumptuous is to be arrogantly or overly bold; it is to take undue liberties; it is the haughty attitude that elbows other people out of the way. It is the opposite of humility.

I remember (as if it were yesterday) the first time I really understood the word *presumptuous*. I was a freshman in college. As I walked into the dormitory from basketball practice one evening, my roommate met me at the door telling me not to be upset. An upperclassman named Barney from down the hall had come into our room, gone through my desk, found my car keys, and "borrowed" my car without asking. Not only that, but Barney had also gone through my closet, picking out and putting on my nicest and newest shirt (one I had never worn because

I was saving it for a special occasion)! Then, he had left, driving my new car and wearing my new shirt. When he returned at midnight, I noticed immediately that he had spilled a chocolate milkshake on my new shirt. As he tossed me the car keys, he told me that my car was down on Highland Avenue, about two blocks away. *He had run out of gas.* Then, as he turned to leave, he told me that I should keep more gas in my car. Now, that's a dramatic example of a presumptuous attitude, and it is not a very pretty picture, is it? I have been thinking recently that it is possible to be presumptuous like that in religion and that we should avoid like the plague any semblance of presumptuous religion. There are indeed some tricky, presumptuous attitudes that we need to beware of in our faith pilgrimage. Let me show you what I mean:

First, beware of presuming that we have all the answers. That is, beware of the arrogant, closed mind; beware of presuming that "my way is the only way." You see, we must keep on growing, stretching, learning. We must be humbly open to new truths from God. To imagine that we have all the answers—how presumptuous that is! God's universe is filled with mystery, and it is the height of haughtiness to close the book on truth.

That's what Jim Jones tried to do. He thought he had all the answers and anyone who differed from him or even questioned him was punished cruelly. That kind of closed mind led to the Guyana tragedy.

Second, beware of presuming that God should bless us at the expense of others. I once heard a high school girl say that she got to be a cheerleader "because one of the other girls fell and broke a leg and that's how God answered my prayer." How presumptuous! To think that God would break the leg of one of his children in order to answer the prayer of another of his children is presumptuous.

Third, beware of presuming people know we love them and appreciate them. The essential sadness is to go through life not loving anybody. The second essential sadness is to love somebody and never get around to telling them.

Fourth, beware of presuming that someone else should uphold the church. Some people want a good church, but they want someone else to see to it. What if every member were exactly like you? What if every member attended as you attend, gave as you gave, and served as you serve? What kind of church would it be?

And fifth, beware of presuming that our wants are more important than God's will. Remember Jesus praying in the Garden of Gethsemane, "Father, . . . not my will but yours be done" (Luke 22:42). In that classic scene, we have the picture of humility . . . and the opposite of presumptuous religion.

LITTLE THINGS MEAN A LOT

There is an old story about a man who walked backwards across the United States. He started in California and ended in New York. At the end of his journey, someone asked him: "What was the hardest part of your trip? Was it the desert or the mountains or the rivers?"

"No," the man answered, "It was the sand in my shoes."

This story has an obvious meaning for most of us in this hectic, busy, stressful world in which we live. We are threatened today far more seriously—in both health and character—by a multitude of little strains than we are by occasional and spectacular ones.

Most of us manage the major emergencies of life in a highly commendable fashion. The great trials—sorrow, tragedy, hardship, bereavement—we handle with poise and strength, only to be worn down and pulled apart by little things.

Think about it. What destroys marriages? Little things! What alienates families? Little things! What is the difference between success and failure? Little things! Nothing determines our destinies more than the way we handle or mishandle little things, the way we cope with "the sand in our shoes."

For example, there are the:

Little worries that can destroy us. There is a lot of wisdom in that prayer, "Lord, we can handle the elephants, but please deliver us from these gnats!"

Little pressures that can stretch us to the breaking point. Some would say that our modern-day civilization's major killers are not heart disease, cancer, and accidents, but calendars, telephones, and clocks—the tyranny of an accelerated, pressurized life.

Little resentments are spiritual cancers. Nothing poisons our souls more quickly than little jealousies. Medical doctors have also discovered that resentment, envy, and jealousy can actually make us physically ill.

These little worries, little pressures, and little resentments can gnaw at us incessantly. So, what do we do? How do we withstand the onslaught? Here are four quick suggestions:

1. Travel light. Decide what is really important to you and give your energies to those things. We can't do everything, so we have to decide what really matters and weed out the rest.

2. Take one step at a time. Live one day at a time. Do one thing at a time. Live in day-tight compartments and celebrate the present.

3. Learn to respond rather than to react. When I react, I am thinking of myself, my wants, my interests, my will. When I respond, I am thinking of others, of a cause, of God.

4. Relax your soul in God. That is, do the best you can and trust God to bring it out right. Be the best person you can be, be faithful to the best you know, and then relax and trust God.

THE POWER OF KINDNESS

Some years ago when I was a seminary student, I served a church in Lithopolis, Ohio. Lithopolis is a small, beautiful village in the center of the state near Columbus.

One summer afternoon as I drove down the main street of that little town, I drove into one of the most memorable experiences of my life.

It was raining steadily. Just ahead of me, I saw a little girl, who looked to be about eight or nine years old, lose control of her bicycle on the rain-slick street and crash to the pavement, scraping her knee and spilling a sack full of groceries in the road.

I stopped to help her. She was crying quietly as I cleaned her injured knee and helped her gather up the scattered groceries.

She willingly accepted my offer to drive her home. We deposited the soggy groceries in the backseat of my car and placed her bike in the trunk. Following her directions, we arrived at her home in only a matter of a few seconds.

Her mother was most gracious and appreciative, that is, until she found out who I was.

When I told her that I was the new Methodist minister in town, her mood changed abruptly. Quickly, so suddenly, she became nervous, almost frightened, and she began to beg me to leave. She blurted out the fact that her husband, who was due home any moment now, didn't like ministers and would not permit any minister to come into their home. Early in his life he had had some bad experience that somehow had caused him to despise the church.

As his wife told me of his hostility toward religion, I noticed that all over the wall were pictures of her husband as a champion boxer. His nickname was "Bruiser." He was a huge man with monstrous arms and fierce eyes. Even as I looked at his pictures and the boxing trophies and ribbons displayed there, I, too, had a sudden mood change. I decided that it probably would be a good idea for me to leave before "Bruiser" got home.

But it was too late. He was coming in the front door. Nervously, his wife stammered out an introduction. As soon as he heard that I was a minister, he looked at me angrily and said, "Get out and don't ever come back. No one from the church is wanted here. No minister is welcome here. Get out right now!"

His wife looked at the floor, embarrassed. And I did what anyone in his right mind would do, I said, "I'm sorry," and then I turned and left.

The next Sunday morning during the first hymn, I couldn't believe my eyes. Bruiser slipped into the back of the church and took a seat on the last pew.

A shocked murmur slid across the congregation. There were a few gasps, numerous whispers, lots of raised eyebrows—and I gulped a couple of times myself.

During the last hymn, Bruiser slipped quietly out of the church. I didn't see him again until the next Sunday when he came back and at the end of the service. He came down to the altar and joined the church on profession of faith. It was a touching moment. People were moved to tears—and I was moved to curiosity.

Which sermon had touched him? This Sunday's? Or the one before? What had broken through that hard shell of hostility? I had to know—so I asked him.

His answer caught me off guard. He said, "Jim, I hate

to tell you this, but it wasn't either of your sermons. It wasn't anything you said."

"Well, what was it then?" I asked. I'll never forget his answer. He said, "You were kind to my little girl. That's what got my attention. You were kind to my daughter."

I learned a valuable lesson that day, a lesson about the importance of kindness.

In fact, one of the most significant and impressive signs of Christian faith is kindness. We don't have to be thoughtless or arrogant or rude or harsh or preoccupied or hateful. We can choose to be kind!

For you see, we may master church history, speak high-sounding theological phrases into the air, quote the great philosophers, even commit to memory large blocks of scripture, but only when we show people genuine kindness do they really begin to see our faith.

If you want to be an effective witness for God, if you want to live daily in the spirit of Christ, if you want to do good for your church, then be a kind person. Be kind to everyone you meet.

HAVE YOU EVER BEEN REDUCED TO A SHAMEFUL SILENCE?

Have you ever been reduced to an embarrassed silence—the kind that comes from a sense of shame, from doing wrong and being found out, from suddenly realizing that you have let down your best self?

There is a haunting example of this kind of embarrassed silence in Mark's Gospel. Remember the story with me.

Jesus is heading toward Jerusalem and toward the cross when his disciples begin to bicker and quarrel about which of them should be greatest in the Kingdom. Can you picture this in your imagination? There is something painfully heartbreaking in this scene.

On the one hand, here is Jesus, moving steadfastly toward the cross, his face set toward Jerusalem, resolved, committed. Surely, he is thinking deep thoughts about the volatile confrontation that was certain to come in the Holy City. He is determined to stand firm, to face it head-on, come what may.

Then, on the other hand, here are the disciples, walking along behind him. They are completely misunderstanding the Kingdom, thinking of it in simplistic, selfish, materialistic terms and of themselves as the prestigious chiefs of state, bickering and quarreling over who should get the most important positions.

They are not aware that Jesus hears them, but he does. Then he stops. He turns and asks them, "What were you discussing with each other as you walked along?" He knows, you see, and now with this incriminating question, they realize that he knows and "they were silent" (see Mark 9:33-34).

Think about that phrase: "they were silent," reduced to the silence of shame, an embarrassed silence, so ashamed of their pettiness that they are speechless.

Isn't it strange how things take their proper place and acquire their true character when they are set before the eyes of Christ, when they are "played back" in the presence of Christ?

So long as the disciples thought Jesus was not hearing them, the argument about who should be greatest seemed fair enough, but when that argument had to be stated in Jesus' presence, it was exposed in all its unworthiness.

This raises a penetrating question: If Christ knew what we were doing, saying, thinking, or feeling, would we be red-faced and speechless?

Be candid with yourself for just a moment. Have you ever been reduced to an embarrassed, shameful silence? I guess if the truth were known, we all have.

I'm thinking of a group of people engaged in a rather cruel gossip session, talking harshly and critically about another person, when suddenly that person walks unannounced into the room—and there is an awkward, embarrassed silence.

I'm thinking of some teenagers thumbing through some questionable literature, when suddenly their mother appears at the door—and there is an awkward, embarrassed silence.

I'm thinking of a group of men exchanging shady stories, when suddenly right in the middle of one of the stories—perhaps at the most profane moment—someone they respect and admire greatly walks up unexpectedly. Again, there is an awkward, shameful silence.

I'm thinking of some office workers who are really loafing on the job, wasting valuable time, when suddenly the boss walks in—and quietly, quickly, abashedly, they slip back into their work places.

Do any of these sound at all familiar? Being caught like that can be a very agonizing experience.

Blow that up a bit, take it deeper, and you have something like what happened to the disciples in Capernaum that day as they traveled with Jesus on the road to Jerusalem.

Their bickering and quarreling, their pettiness and jealousy, their selfishness and hostility came back to haunt them. Deep down they knew that these destructive attitudes did not really fit in his Kingdom. That is why the disciples were reduced to a shameful silence when they were exposed.

Think about this. There is a certain pathos about this. The disciples were quarreling, bickering, fussing, and backbiting. Even as Jesus, the master of love, moves intently toward the cross, his closest followers, his most intimate friends, are seething with jealousy, hostility, and selfishness.

Time and again, they have heard him teach love. They have seen his acts of loving-kindness and yet they have missed his main point. Jesus had to go to the cross to get their attention! There on the cross he shows them (and us) that love (not hostility or jealousy or selfishness) is life as God meant it to be.

This quarreling of the disciples bothers Jesus very much and so he stops to deal with it seriously. He teaches them again to be servants, to be humble, to be trusting, and to be loving, caring, compassionate persons.

Jesus is disturbed by their selfish attitudes with good reason. It's because he knows that these same things magnified, blown up to a larger scale, await him in Jerusalem. A scant few days later, these same destructive attitudes would conspire to nail him to a cross.

Sadly, it is still happening. Today, every time we demonstrate these destructive, selfish attitudes, we are crucifying God's truth and somewhere along the way we have to answer for it. But the good news is that God's truth cannot be killed. It resurrects!

Ultimately, God's truth and love win the day. Then bickering and quarreling, pettiness and jealousy, selfishness and hostility will forever be reduced to a shameful silence.

THE AMAZING SERENITY
OF JESUS

One of the most impressive emblems of Holy Week
is the serenity of Jesus in those difficult hours and
days that led to the cross. His strength of character is
nothing short of amazing.

His deep sense of peace, his quiet confidence, his inner calm, his courage, his serenity of spirit—whatever
you want to call it, that quality of poise and composure
stands out vividly.

We see it even more dramatically as the gospel writers set it alongside the nervous personality of Pontius
Pilate. Focus on that dramatic scene where Jesus stands
on trial before Pilate, the Roman governor. What a contrast! How different these two men are!

If you asked someone who knew nothing of the story
to point out the "strong one" in this scene—using our

present-day standards for measuring strength—he or she would point quickly to Pilate. He or she would justify the choice by underscoring Pilate's wealth, his position, his power, his authority, his political clout, his fame—and yet he or she would be wrong, so very wrong!

Who has the inner peace and real strength here? Not Pilate! He has the outer circumstances, but not the inner stability. It's obvious, as you look closer, that Jesus is the strong one here. In fact, his inner strength and serenity completely baffle Pilate.

First, look at Pilate. He's confused, upset, and weak. He can't make up his mind. In a dither, he runs from one group to the other, asking questions here and there. He tries to pass the buck to Herod. He knows that Jesus is innocent, but he does not have the strength of character to stand firm for what is right. This is the picture of a man who is running scared!

Outwardly, Pilate has it all: power, wealth, position, fame. But inwardly, where it counts, he's scared to death, nervous as a long-tailed cat in a room full of rocking chairs!

Finally, he washes his hands, trying to straddle the fence. Like a nervous politician, he gives the people what they want—he turns Jesus over to them for execution.

But, then, just in case someone else may see it differently, he tries to act as if he is not involved.

Is that strength of character? Is that peace of mind? Is that serenity of spirit? Is being scared, confused, and weak the picture of strength? Of course not!

Then look at Jesus. He stands there poised, confident, unafraid, and serene. He is facing death, but his strength never wavers. Just think of it: an unfair trial for an innocent man; lies, plotting, conniving; jealousy, hostility, hatred; a mob scene and a kangaroo court. And in the face of it all, Jesus exhibits an incredible quality of inner peace, strength, and calm.

They betray him, deny him, taunt him, beat him, curse him, spit on him, and nail him to a cross. And he says: "Father, forgive them; for they do not know what they are doing" (Luke 23:34).

That is strength of character, isn't it? That is inner peace and spiritual power.

Now, the question is, What produced that amazing strength of character and moral fiber in Jesus? Simply this:

He knew who he was!
He knew where he was going!
He knew who was with him!

IS THERE ANY HOPE?

We are living in desperate times, in a world that breeds cynicism and despair.

Read the morning paper or watch the evening news and you will find story after story of crimes, murders, robberies, assaults, violence, political unrest, rumors of war, the cost of living escalating, and the dollar shrinking.

It's enough to make Norman Vincent Peal a pessimist!

In this kind of crazy, troubled world, we do have to be careful. We do have to be cautious. We do have to be wary. But we dare not become paranoid. We dare not become somber cynics. We must not give in to a scared, depressed pessimism. We must not lose hope!

The question is: How do we believe the best things in the worst times? How can we hold on to the miracle of hope? How can we keep on trusting and hoping and believing the best in such strange, violent, desperate times?

Some years ago, a U.S. submarine sank off the coast of Massachusetts, becoming a prison for its crew. Ships were rushed to the scene to attempt a rescue. Deep-sea divers went to see if anything could be done. The men in the submarine clung desperately to life, waiting to be rescued.

Slowly, but surely, their oxygen supply was running out. The divers outside the sub and the frightened men inside communicated with each other by tapping Morse code on the wall of the submarine. Time was running out and they knew it.

After a seemingly long pause, a question was slowly tapped out from inside the submarine: "Is there any hope?"

"Is there any hope?" That is the question each of us will have to ask and answer at some point in life. Many are asking it now in these desperate times.

Cervantes, in his novel *Don Quixote*, answers the question for us as he says, "While there's life, there's hope!" The great people of faith have always believed that. They have always been people of hope.

Moses—caught between pharaoh's army and the deep Red Sea in a seemingly hopeless situation—went forward and trusted God to open a way.

Shadrach, Meshach, and Abednego went into the fiery furnace—into a seemingly hopeless situation—and they trusted God to be with them and he was.

David stood before Goliath. What chance could a little boy with a slingshot have against this giant of a warrior? But David believed that God was with him and it made all the difference.

The Apostle Paul was a master in the art of hopeful living. He knew how to handle opposing circumstances, how to overcome handicaps, and how to take the hard situations of life and turn them to good.

Toward the end of his life, he was arrested and put in prison. He was separated from his friends, cut off from his dream of going to Spain. He was sick and faced death. Talk about a hopeless situation!

Who would have blamed Paul if he had given up? But look at how he handled it. He refused to give in to self-pity. He refused to give in to disillusionment. He refused to give in to bitterness. He refused to quit. He kept on believing, trusting, and hoping.

Remember Jesus. He taught hope. He lived it. He died for it. Just think of it. They betrayed him and nailed him to a cross. And He kept believing in people and the Father.

Jesus knew as much about the hard knocks of life as the cynics know. He knew that people could be cruel. He knew that life can be unfair. But nowhere does he give up on people, nowhere does he quit on life, nowhere does he run out on God.

Jesus, in his life and teachings and death, calls us to be people of hope, people who believe, people who believe the best things in the worst times—people who hang on to the miracle of hope in a desperate world.

SPIRITUAL MATURITY

The imminent psychiatrist Dr. G. B. Chisholm once made a significant and provocative statement that is something to think about. He said: "So far in the history of the world, there have never been enough mature people in the right places."

That is a real problem, isn't it? We settle for childishness rather than pay the price for maturity. Just think of it.

In politics, how childish we have become. A candidate promises mature leadership and then spends the entire campaign attacking his opponent with ugly smear tactics and never getting around to the real issues. In a recent local election, I voted in every race but one. When I got in the voting booth, I could not bring myself to vote for either candidate, because I felt that they both had been so embarrassingly childish.

Then what about international affairs? One nation says to another, "If you don't do what I want you to do, then I won't talk to you anymore!" How childish we have become!

Or how about entertainment? Picture this. You are driving along when suddenly over the car radio comes a smooth, suave voice telling you about a new form of entertainment that has come to town. "It is entertainment not for everybody," the voice assures you. "It is entertainment that is mature, sophisticated, thought-provoking entertainment designed for intelligent audiences." You are very interested in this until you realize that the announcer is plugging a new movie at the drive-in called "Sex Kittens on College Campus." What could be more childish!

Jesus saw the dangers and problems connected with this kind of childish immaturity and much of his teaching can be capsuled to mean, "Grow up! Don't act like spoiled children! Be mature!" With that in mind let me quickly outline some characteristics of spiritual maturity:

First, the spiritually mature person knows how to handle frustration, knows how to deal with disappointments, how to turn problems into opportunities and defeats into victories. If a child does not get the toy he wants, the child will scream, cry, throw something, scratch or bite or hit.

Put that kind of immature response to frustration on a bigger stage and it can be devastating. It makes you wonder, doesn't it? How many lives have been lost, wars started, families alienated, marriages destroyed, communities disrupted, persons hurt because of childish, immature people who have not learned how to handle frustration?

Second, the spiritually mature person knows how to take responsibility for his or her own life. Childish people expect special favors, want somebody else to do things for them, and blame others when things don't go their way. Mature people take charge of their own lives.

Third, the spiritually mature person knows how to forgive. Childish people want to get even. Mature people want to forgive! If you ever wonder, "Should I forgive that person who has hurt me or wronged me?" If that question ever comes to your mind, then just remember the picture of Jesus hanging on the cross and saying: "Father, forgive them." That is our measuring stick for forgiveness and for maturity.

Fourth, the spiritually mature person knows how to be self-giving. Childish people are selfish. Mature people are loving. A paraphrase of the Apostle Paul's words in the love chapter says it all: "Put away childish things. Grow up and learn how to love. The greatest of these, the most mature of these, is love" (1 Corinthians 13, paraphrased).

THREE STAGES OF LIFE

In growing up, we normally pass through three stages of life that may be represented as follows:

1. The Childish Stage, where the cry is "Please do something for me!"

2. The Adolescent Stage, where the cry is "Please leave me alone. I can take care of myself," and

3. The Mature Adult Stage, where the cry is "Please let me do something for you. Please let me be a servant for others!"

To get into this a little deeper, let's look together at each of these stages and their unique characteristics.

Look first at the childish stage. The key word here is *selfishness*. The attitude here is an immature disregard for others. Remember how Paul put it: "When I was a child, I spoke like a child, I thought like a child, I reasoned like a child; when I became an adult, I put an end to childish ways" (1 Corinthians 13:11).

Now, life brings no greater blessing than a child. Obviously, children are wonderful, but it is a heartbreaking tragedy for a child to never develop physically, mentally, socially, emotionally, or spiritually. And the truth is some people never mature. Let me show you what I mean. Look at the characteristics of childish persons.

Childish people become very upset over any personal hurt. If a pin sticks, they will cry as if deadly wounded. They are not concerned about the suffering of others. Childish people weep mostly for themselves.

Also, childish people want to be the center of attention. They are jealous of all those around them. They are willing to play, but only if they can choose the game. They demand applause and appreciation.

In addition, childish people have to be taught to be thankful. Gratitude is not something that is evident in their lives. They take the blessings of life for granted, as a matter of course, as something they are due.

Childish people think they owe no one anything. Their attitude is to get all they can for themselves with little sense of obligation to anyone. They rarely think of what they owe their parents or their coworkers or the society in which they live.

Childish people are completely self-centered. They live twenty-four hours a day in a world that revolves around them.

Childishness is pettiness. It is immature selfishness. The cry of the childish person is "Please do something for me! Please help me! Please give me something!"

Next, look at the adolescent stage. The key word is *arrogance*, but other descriptive adjectives fly fast and furious: rebellious, restless, discontent, ruthless, prideful.

Adolescent people are those who went overboard in trying to cut the apron strings. They let the pendulum swing too far and they have become hostile and resentful of any authority over their lives.

This is an older version of the "terrible twos." Many teenagers go through this reaction to authority as they develop, but then they settle back. Adolescent people are those who never have swung back. They are scared to death, but they try to cover up by saying loudly over and over things such as:

"I don't answer to anybody. I'm my own boss."

"Nobody's gonna tell me how to behave."

"My life's my own, and I'll do as I please."

"You gotta look out for number one."

"I know what I want to get out of life, and nobody is going to stop me."

"I'm a self-made man."

"I don't need anybody."

Adolescent people say these kinds of things over and over and so loudly that you wonder who they are trying to convince.

One biblical illustration of the adolescent stage is the picture of Adam and Eve saying, in effect: "Who does God think he is telling us what we can eat and what we can't eat?"

The word here is *arrogance* and the cry of the adolescent person is "Please leave me alone. I can take care of myself."

Now, look at the mature adult stage. The key here is humble service or gracious thoughtfulness. Mature people are big-spirited, magnanimous, tender, concerned, and committed to others in goodwill.

They weep mostly for others. They appreciate approval, but work on even when there is no recognition. They are saturated with the spirit of gratitude. They are filled with the spirit of compassion.

It's interesting to note that both Jesus and Paul equated maturity with love. Throughout his life and teachings, Jesus encouraged us in words and deeds to be merciful like God. "Blessed are the merciful," he said in Matthew 5:7. Paul said: "The greatest of these [the most mature of these] is love" (1 Corinthians 13:13).

The most mature person, then, is the person most able to be loving—and the cry here is "Please let me do something for you. Let me be a friend and neighbor and servant to others."

In conclusion, consider these two quick observations:

First, don't categorize people. Don't say "Nancy is so childish" and "Look at Bill, he is so adolescent," and of course, "I am mature!" No, that is not helpful because, you see, the truth is that these three potentialities are within each of us all the time. At any given moment, I may be childish, adolescent, or mature.

Second, the Christian faith says "grow up." The way to grow up and become mature is to become more loving!

MAGNANIMITY— THE ESSENTIAL SPIRIT OF THE CHRISTIAN

One of the highest compliments we can give some-one is to call him or her a magnanimous person. Some would appropriately call magnanimity the noblest of human graces.

Magnanimity. What does it mean?

Well, it's a million-dollar word for a much, much richer spirit. The dictionary defines it as the "quality of being big in spirit, gentle, kind, considerate, rising above pettiness or meanness, forgiving, gracious and generous in overlooking injury or insult."

The Apostle Paul, writing a long time ago to his friends at Philippi, called the spirit of magnanimity the essential spirit of the Christian. He told the Philippians that a Christian should be characterized by his or her magnanimity and that this bigness of spirit should be obvious to others, not silent and secretive but radiant and infectious, as bright as the sunlight and as loud as the rushing wind.

"Let your magnanimity be manifest to all," said Paul (Philippians 4:5, paraphrased). But, what is magnanimity? Let me try to paint its picture.

We see it in Abraham Lincoln. He was a big man, a man big in spirit. He showed marvelous magnanimity, especially toward General McClellan, whom he appointed to command the armies of the North in the Civil War.

McClellan was a brash, young upstart, an obnoxious man who treated President Lincoln terribly, yet because Lincoln respected and trusted McClellan as a soldier, he suffered his personal insults patiently.

One evening, Lincoln and a colleague went to Mc-Clellan's home on a matter of great urgency concerning the war. Of course, people normally go to the president, but Lincoln—trying to be friendly and wanting not to inconvenience McClellan—came to his home.

After keeping the president waiting for a long time, McClellan sent word down by a servant that he was just too tired to see Lincoln. Lincoln's colleague was indignant; the other cabinet members wanted McClellan kicked out immediately for this insubordination and rudeness.

But Lincoln replied that he would "gladly hold McClellan's horse if he would only win the battles" (Henry Ketcham, *The Life of Abraham Lincoln*). That's magnanimity!

Earlier Edwin Stanton had publicly denounced Lincoln as a "fool." Stanton called him a "low, cunning clown" and he referred to him as "the original gorilla." So what did the president do? He appointed Stanton the Secretary of War because he saw Stanton as the best man for the job! That's magnanimity!

We see it in that famous poem, "Outwitted," written by Edwin Markham:

> He drew a circle that shut me out—
> Heretic, rebel, a thing to flout.
> But Love and I had the wit to win:
> We drew a circle that took him in.

That's magnanimity.

We see it in Booker T. Washington, the great African American educator. One day as Professor Washington was walking to work at the famous Tuskegee Institute in Alabama, he happened to pass the mansion of a wealthy woman.

The woman didn't recognize him and she called out to him: "Hey, you! Come here. I need some wood chopped!" Without a word, Washington peeled off his jacket, picked up the ax, and went to work. He not only cut a large pile of wood but also carried the firewood into the house and arranged it neatly.

He had scarcely left when a servant said to the woman: "I guess you didn't recognize him, ma'am, but that was Professor Washington!" Embarrassed, ashamed, and red-faced, the woman hurried over to Tuskegee Institute to apologize.

Washington replied: "There's no need to apologize, madam. I'm delighted to do favors for my friends!"

That's magnanimity!

We see it in this classic definition of a saint. Someone once asked: "What made the saints, saints?"

This was the answer given: "Because they were cheerful when it was difficult to be cheerful; patient when it was difficult to be patient; and, because they pushed on when they wanted to stand still and kept silent when they wanted to talk and were agreeable when they wanted to be disagreeable."

That was all. It was quite simple really and always will be—and that's magnanimity!

Of course, we see the best portrait of magnanimity in Jesus Christ. He taught it in the Sermon on the Mount:

"Go the second mile," he said "Turn the other cheek. Give him your cloak as well as your coat. Love your enemies. Pray for those who persecute you. Be merciful like your Father in heaven" (Matthew 5:39-48, paraphrased). That's magnanimity.

He didn't just teach it and talk about it. More than that, he lived magnanimously! Think of it:

Jesus saying, "Let the little children come," and then taking them up in his arms (Matthew 19:14).

Jesus saying to the woman taken in adultery, "Neither do I condemn you. Go your way, and from now on do not sin again" (John 8:11).

Jesus on the cross praying, "Father, forgive them; for they do not know what they are doing" (Luke 23:34).

That's magnanimity and it's a good word for our vocabularies and a great spirit for our lives.

THE BEST QUALITIES IN LIFE ARE REFLECTIONS OF GOD

It took Alex Haley twelve years to do it—twelve years to research it and write it—but finally in 1976, he completed his book. It was entitled *Roots: The Saga of an American Family.*

In this epic work, which some believe is destined to become a classic of American literature, Haley traces his family's origins back to their roots in a drama spanning two centuries—from the African Kunta Kinte through the six generations that came after him to Alex Haley and the present day.

During the last television segment, there was a powerful and poignant scene. Remember it: Tom Murray, the son of Chicken George, is preparing to take his family to freedom in Tennessee when Major Cates, who has treated them so terribly, comes out to try to stop them. Cates has cursed them, beaten them, abused them, and overworked them with horrendous cruelty—especially Tom Murray.

Cates always seemed to have it in for Tom, and on at least one occasion he flogged Tom almost to death with a whip.

Now, when Cates tries to stop them, the slaves—with the thirst for freedom in their hearts—turn on him. They capture him. They tie him to the whipping post. And they bring a whip to Tom so Tom can "pay him back" for the brutalizing thing Cates has done.

Cates pleads for mercy. Cates—the one who has been so cruel, so hateful, so mean to them—now pleads for mercy.

Holding the whip tightly in his hand, Tom looks at Cates tied to the whipping post. He hears Cates whimpering and begging for compassion. If ever a man deserved to be flogged, it was Cates. Here was Tom's chance to unleash two centuries of his family's hurt and heartache and frustration.

And yet as our family watched that scene together, I found myself saying out loud: "I hope he doesn't whip him. I'm going to be disappointed if he beats him." Then our daughter, Jodi, said: "Don't worry, Dad. He won't. It just wouldn't fit his character."

Just about that time, Tom Murray drops the whip to the ground, turns, and walks away. He refuses to beat Cates. Cates falls to his knees at the whipping post and cries in relief.

I felt relieved, too. I would have been let down if Tom had beaten him. Tom had been there. He knew what it felt like. And in that tense moment, compassion had won the day.

I thought to myself, *That is beautiful!* The quality of mercy is indeed beautiful. It is so much better than vengeance or hostility. Then I realized that this is precisely what Jesus believed, taught, lived for, and what he died for.

Since that time, I have realized even more deeply that the best qualities we know in life are reflections of God. Let me express that again: The best qualities we know in life, the best actions, are reflections of the spirit of God.

For example, we know from our own personal experience that some attitudes are better than others. The word *better* here may mean "more Godlike." To say that love is better than hate, that mercy is better than cruelty, that empathy is better than jealousy is just another way of saying that love, mercy, and empathy are of God. They are more Godlike! When we express these kinds of attitudes, we are reflecting God.

THE HEALING POWER
OF THE CHURCH

We were never meant to bear our burdens alone. We were never meant to suffer in isolation. It is the genius of the Christian faith that it recognizes this truth.

We in the church family are a community of love sharing the joys and sorrows of life together from the cradle to the grave. The anthem "No Man Is an Island" is based on John Donne's famous words, and it reminds us powerfully that we all need one another, that not one of us is an island, that none of us stand alone, that we are all brothers and sisters with God as our Father.

You see, we solve our problems better in community than in isolation. We all need a "support community." We need a support system to affirm us, to uphold us, to love us, to encourage us, and that is a significant part of the task of the church.

The scriptures put it like this: "Bear ye one another's burdens" (Galatians 6:2 KJV).

There was a woman who had not been to church for some time. Her minister saw her and told her that she had been missed. She replied, "Well, I've got some problems right now that I'm dealing with. As soon as I get on top of them, then I'll be back to church."

The minister answered: "But don't you see that's not the way it works? You need us now more than you ever did."

The church should be the place of encouragement. Tragically, many people make a bad mistake at this point. For example, I was visiting recently with a grief-stricken woman whose husband had died some months before. She was struggling, downcast, despondent. Part of her problem was that she had stayed away from church.

"The church was so special to us," she said. "I couldn't bear to go back without him."

But, you see, that's a mistake. The church should be a part of the healing process. It's our support system, and when the heartache comes, we need to get back to the church as quickly as we can. Let me illustrate that.

On December 17, 1979, my mother was killed instantly in an automobile accident in Winston-Salem,

North Carolina. The funeral was held in Memphis on December 20. We had to stay over a few days longer to handle some family and business matters. We flew back into Shreveport on Christmas Eve, still very much in shock and grieving deeply.

We landed at 3:30 that Christmas Eve afternoon, drove to our home, put our luggage in the house, looked quickly at the mail—and headed for the church for the Christmas Eve communion service.

This was a very emotional moment for me—our first time back in the church since my mother's funeral.

I will never forget what happened that night as long as I live. It was one of the most moving spiritual experiences of my life. During the communion service, as I moved up and down the altar rail, serving the Holy Communion bread tray, people would reach and touch my hands! They didn't say anything. They would just touch my hands. Even now, as I write this, my eyes water as I think of it.

That had never happened before or since—hundreds of people (from the smallest child to the oldest adult) just touching my hands—saying nothing verbally, but saying oh so much with the gentle touch of encouragement.

It was a powerful moment for me. I had never felt more loved or more encouraged. Now, that is what the church is all about!

CELEBRATING THE JOY OF THE JOURNEY

Is it possible that we get so caught up in our dream of a happy ending that we miss the joy of the journey?

Could it be that we sometimes look so intently for some promised land tucked away in the distant future that we become blind to what we already have at our fingertips?

Let's think together about that for a few moments by considering these three thoughts:

First, the truth is that we all know some unhappy endings. We all experience some disappointments, some frustrations, some uncompleted tasks.

Some years ago, a young left-handed pitcher broke into the major leagues of professional baseball. He was so talented that he quickly made headlines with his scorching fastball. He became an all-star in his rookie season and was destined to become one of the greatest pitchers of all time.

However, early in his career, during the off-season, he slipped while mowing his lawn barefooted. His foot went under the mower and was severely cut. He underwent surgery and his foot healed, but somehow the accident affected his stride, and his fastball was never the same.

In a few short months, he realized that he couldn't make a comeback, and he dropped out of baseball while still in his early twenties.

He could relate, I'm sure, to Moses, who was so near the promised land but only glimpsed it from afar. Remember Moses—and how abruptly his story ends. For forty years he had dreamed of it, but then Moses died before they got there, a stone's throw short of his goal and lifelong dream, he died!

Does this seem fair? Was Moses's life a failure?

Or, is it possible that though Moses never reached the land physically, he had been there in his heart, mind, and soul all along? You see, the truth is that Moses had possessed the promised land all along. He had it in his heart. He had seen it, felt it, dreamed it, loved it all along.

This brings us to the second thought, that happy endings are fine, but don't forget that *there is great joy in the journey.* This is a very important lesson to learn from Moses, isn't it? The real promised lands are within us. We don't have to wait for the "sweet by and by." We can have the joy of the journey now.

Indeed, Moses's victory was in the journey. That's where he found the Ten Commandments. That's where he shaped that motley crew of slaves into God's servant people. That's where he made his impact on human history.

The bigger part of Moses's story was the traveling, not the arriving.

So, the lesson for us is clear: Stop and smell the roses! Celebrate the present! Relish the moment! Feel God's spirit within you now! Seize the joy of the journey today, and trust God for tomorrow!

One more thing remains to be said: *nothing that is really great and important is ever finished in one generation.* Each person dies with something undone.

We never do all we want to do. We never do all we intend to do. We never see all we hope to see.

So, we have to learn the hard lessons of patience and trust. We must do what we can and then trust others— and God—to see that what we have begun will be continued. We do our best and then trust others to take up the torch.

Remember how Brother Adrian put it as he spoke of Jesus: "He came singing love. He lived singing love. He died singing love. He rose in silence. If the song is to continue, we must do the singing."

THE DANGERS OF THE BLAME GAME

Isn't it interesting how, when something goes wrong, the first thing we want to do is find someone to blame it on?

Look at the Israelites at the Red Sea. They see that cloud of dust on the horizon being kicked up by pharaoh's army and immediately they turn on Moses. Moments ago, he was their champion, their leader, their hero. But now, when trouble rears its head, they go for the jugular. "It's all your fault, Moses! A fine mess you've gotten us into. Why did we ever listen to you? You're the one to blame for this."

Some years ago, I had a poignant experience working with an alcoholic. I'll call him Lloyd. He had been drunk and missing for thirty-eight days. He had left home drunk on Christmas Eve. He staggered back home on January 31. His wife called me and asked me to go up to the house to check on him.

When I knocked on the door, I heard a lamp crash to the floor inside. He was stumbling and falling around in a drunken stupor. I knocked again and called out his name. I heard him fall to the floor and begin to crawl toward the front door. He fumbled around with the doorknob and finally pushed the door open.

Can you imagine this scene? As the door opened, he was lying there on his stomach on the floor and he saw my feet. Slowly he turned his head upward and he found himself looking into the face of his minister. I guess at that moment I must have looked ten feet tall to him—because he was dirty, he was covered with the filth of his own drunkenness, and he had not washed, shaved, or changed clothes for over a month.

He began to cry. I helped him up and got him on the couch. I washed his face with a warm washcloth and began to try to get some food and coffee into him.

Suddenly, he turned on me. He blamed me for his problem. Then he blamed his wife and then his parents. Then he started in on his neighbors and those "hypocrites" down at the church. He blamed the mayor, the president, and the Congress. He even cursed God for letting him be born. And I just sat there and listened.

Finally, he turned back to me and said, "Jim, aren't you going to say anything?"

And I said, "Well, Lloyd, I'm just sitting here trying to think if there is anybody else we could come up with to blame this on."

He looked at me angrily, and for a moment I thought I had gone too far. But, then, he looked down at his feet and, after a few moments of silence, he said, "It's all my fault! I've made such a mess of my life, haven't I?"

"Well," I answered, "you are a mess right now, but your life is not over. You can start over again."

Lloyd paused for a moment and then he said, "Jim, do you really believe that? Do you really believe that God can help me to whip this thing?"

And I said to him, "I surely do, Lloyd. But the real question is do you believe it? And are you ready to do something about it? Are you ready to admit that you've got a problem and that you need help?"

Evidently he was, because we got him professional help. We got him to Alcoholics Anonymous. And now, with their help, with his church's help, with his family's help—and with God's help—he is whipping alcoholism.

He called me the other day. He hasn't had a drink in over eighteen years. He is serving this year as chairman of the board for his church and as a youth counselor.

He knows that he still has a problem. He knows that he is one drink away from big trouble. But he also knows that he can't blame anybody else anymore and that when he takes responsibility for his own life, his community will help him, his family will help him, his church will help him, and God will help him too.

FIVE DIFFERENT WAYS
TO LEARN THE TRUTH

Broadly speaking, we learn the truth in five different ways:

First, we learn directly through command, rule, law, or authoritative statement. This is our earliest brush with truth. Very early in life, some authoritative people begin to teach us about life. They tell us directly, straight-out, what is appropriate and what is not.

Directly, we are taught common courtesy: "Say please." Directly, we are taught facts: "Two plus two equals four." Directly, we are taught religion: "Thou shalt not steal."

Notice that direct truth descends upon us. We don't discover truth here ourselves. It is drilled into us. Like computers, we are programmed. Rules, laws, commands, traditions—hundreds of them—are stored away in our brains, and they enable us to survive and to become civilized.

Direct learning is our earliest way of learning. It is also the shallowest—and the most childish—way to learn the truth. It is essential, but it is also the most superficial road to truth because not much thinking happened here. The rules are rarely explained. The authority figure gives the command. We hear it, accept it, and obey it with very little thought.

We need to be taught some things directly. This represents the first step toward truth, but for the truth to become our truth, our own possession, our own commitment, we must move beyond this plateau.

Second, we learn indirectly through parables or stories that slip up on us, surprise us, turn our world upside down, and make us think and rethink!

As we grow and mature, we begin to realize that we can't trust what everybody says to us or tells us. Some things told to us as gospel truth don't pan out.

For example, we may be told that if we use a certain cologne we will be as irresistible as Brad Pitt. But then we discover that it doesn't quite work that way.

We have bumped into the credibility gap, and we become suspicious, maybe even a little cynical. Thus, we don't listen attentively anymore to direct truth. We become fixed in our own attitudes and we tune out.

When this happens, if someone then wants to convey truth to us, they have to use the indirect approach. They tell us a story or a parable with a truth hidden in it, a story that slips up on us, a story that comes around our suspicions, thrusts a mirror in our faces, and says: "That's you! Here is your truth!"—a story that explodes into our neat little world and makes us think.

Third, we learn scientifically through testing ideas and drawing conclusions from our experiments. We hear an idea, we test it, and then we test it again and again. From this process, we learn through experimentation what we can count on and accept. The caution here is that some people get so carried away that they think this is the only road to truth.

Fourth, we learn incarnately through other people. Incarnate truth is truth personified, truth wrapped up in a person. We do tend to learn from other personalities, becoming like some who impress us and trying desperately not to become like others, whose actions we question or find offensive.

In Christian faith, when we speak of the incarnation, we mean that God's truth, God's will, God's idea, or God's intention can be uniquely seen in Jesus Christ. He was God's truth become flesh. In him, we see God's truth incarnate, God's truth wrapped up in a person.

Fifth, we learn experientially through our own personal experience when something happens to us personally that verifies, dramatizes, or underscores a great truth. When someone says experience is the best teacher, he or she means nothing makes truth come alive for us more than does experience.

For example, all my life I heard that honey tasted good, but that really only came alive for me when I tasted it. All my life I heard about being a parent, but I didn't really own that truth until I experienced it for myself.

As we move along in our search for truth, we learn some of God's truth directly through rules, some indirectly through parables, some scientifically through testing, some incarnately through people—but most powerfully we learn through our own personal experiences, through tasting things firsthand. The psalmist knew this, and that's why he said: "O taste and see that the Lord is good; / happy are those who take refuge in him" (34:8).

AGENTS OF FORGIVENESS

Paul Tournier was a Swiss physician and writer who was highly respected all over the world. Someone once described him as skilled in medicine and wise toward God. Dr. Tournier wrote perceptively about the spirit of judgment that fills the world and crowds out the spirit of forgiveness. In one of his books, Dr. Tournier said, "Because recriminations and reproach fill the world, everyone feels under constant criticism, or at any rate threatened with judgment, and he fears its repercussions. No one is indifferent to it; all are hurt by some words, by some look or some opinion contrary to their own. Yet, this fear of being judged is intense and universal . . . even overwhelming."

Dr. Tournier was right. We do live in a world where the spirit of critical judgment consumes us.

We have enough judges, enough criticizers. Indeed, there are too many debunkers. We need forgivers! We need encouragers! We need reconcilers! We need persons committed to the spirit of grace, mercy, compassion, kindness, and love. We need persons determined to let the forgiving spirit be the overriding tone of their lives.

With that in mind, let me make some practical suggestions for helping us become agents of forgiveness.

First, remember to speak the truth in love. There are many ways to speak the truth. You can speak the truth in cruelty or with hatefulness or with hostility. You can speak the truth in a self-righteous manner or in an arrogant tone or with an "I told you so" glance. You can speak the truth in a way that divides people or puts people down. But the Scriptures tell us to speak the truth in love—to speak the truth so that it builds up and doesn't tear apart.

Second, remember that people are more important than pride or principles or things. Whenever you hear yourself say "I will not swallow my pride and say I'm sorry," you can be sure that you have departed from the spirit of Christ.

Whenever you invoke a principle to keep from bringing help or healing to someone, then you can be sure that you have forgotten the example of Jesus, who never

let a law or principle get in his way when he saw someone in trouble.

Whenever you let any material thing separate you
from another person, you can be sure that you have left
the teachings of Christ.

Third, remember to forgive—and forget. Recall Clara
Barton's famous line. When she was reminded of a bad
thing done to her some time earlier, she answered: "I
distinctly remember forgetting that!"

Fourth, remember also that the price of not forgiving can be extremely high. That price can be loneliness
or self-pity or brooding bitterness—or even physical illness. The price of our unbending refusals to forgive can
be fearsomely high, both physically and spiritually.

Fifth, remember that God alone is fit to judge. Our human judgments are so limited, and sometimes so blind.
We just don't have all the facts. We can't always see that
complete picture. Everybody has problems and handicaps of some kind that affect what they do. We don't
always know about those handicaps or those unique
problems. We can't always see them. But God knows
and sees. Only God knows all the truth and only God is
fit to judge fairly and lovingly.

Sixth, remember Jesus on the cross. Look what they
did to him. He was falsely accused, criticized, maligned,

arrested, beaten, scorned, ridiculed, cursed, taunted, and nailed to a cross—and he said, "Father, forgive them!"

That is the measuring stick for forgiveness. That is our example. If you ever wonder, "Should I forgive?"—then remember Jesus on the cross saying, "Father, forgive!"

VICARIOUS LESSONS FROM THE FOOT OF THE CROSS

Educators tell us that we can learn vicariously, that is, through the experiences of others. The truth is that we do tend to learn from other personalities: learning how to act and how not to act, learning how to treat others and how not to treat others, learning how to work and how not to work, becoming like someone who impresses or inspires us and trying desperately not to become like others whose personalities we find objectionable.

When we look at the intriguing cast of characters who come into focus at the crucifixion of Jesus, we discover some fascinating vicarious lessons, some key insights that have the ring of universal truth. From the personalities clustered around the cross, there are some great and timeless lessons to be learned through their experiences. Let me show you what I mean.

First, we look at Herod and see that selfishness is destructive. In Herod, we see how destructive and cruel self-centeredness can be. Remember how Herod refused to take Jesus seriously? He was much too caught up in his own selfish interests. He tried to make a joke of the whole thing! He jested at Jesus. He put a purple robe on Jesus, mocked him, treated him contemptuously, and, with the loud laughter of a selfish, spoiled king, he sent him back to Pilate and to a cross. How could anyone so important as Herod be bothered with a peasant carpenter from Nazareth?

It is interesting to note that earlier Jesus had referred to Herod as "the fox." It was a fitting name for Herod because a fox is a beast of prey. It lives off the bodies of others. It takes without giving. It can be cruel, cunning, tricky, and heartless—the symbol of selfishness.

Remember Herod the fox: how he stole away his brother's wife, how he beheaded John the Baptist, how he mocked and taunted Jesus.

What about us? Can we learn a lesson from Herod? Does our selfishness cause other people to be hurt? Are we so busy "playing king" that we can't recognize the King of kings when he walks into our presence?

Second, we look at Judas and see that a good start is not enough. We have to finish; we have to persevere; we have to see it through. Judas started out so well. He had so much promise. Jesus called him. The other disciples liked him and trusted him. They made him treasurer of the group. But something went wrong. He quit. He betrayed his Lord, and today no name in history is as despised as the name of Judas Iscariot—because even though he made a good start, he didn't finish well. It's so important to finish what you start.

What about us: Can we learn a vicarious lesson from Judas? Do we realize the importance of seeing things through?

Third, we look at Pilate and see that indifference won't work. You just can't sit on the fence. Pilate tried to wash his hands of Christ, but he couldn't do it. He tried to pass the buck, but couldn't. He tried to act innocent, but couldn't. After all these years, his hands are still stained.

Can we learn from Pilate that indifference will not work, that we must stand for something lest we fall for everything?

Fourth, we look at Simon Peter and see that no failure need be final. The good news of our faith—and the experience of Peter—is that you can start over, you can make a comeback, you can be forgiven. It's not the falling down; it's the staying down that ruins you. This was the difference between Judas and Peter. Both failed, but Judas thought his failure was final and he quit altogether. But Peter bounced back and became a committed and courageous leader.

Can we learn from Peter that even when we fail, we can make a comeback?

Fifth, we look at Jesus and see that love is the greatest and most powerful thing in the world. We see him in the Upper Room saying, "I give you a new commandment, that you love one another. Just as I have loved you, you also should love one another. By this everyone will know that you are my disciples, if you have love for one another" (John 13:34-35).

From Jesus, we learn the most valuable lesson of all—that love is the best thing in the world.

THE CALLING

Remember Margaret Deeney's poem called "The Greatest Words." In it she reminds us of some of the nicest compliments we hear in life, such as "I love you" or "Will you marry me?" but then she concludes her poem with these two poignant lines:

> But the greatest words in all the world (are)
> "I've got a job for you!"

Let me illustrate that personally by telling you about my own call to the ministry.

Let me preface what I am about to say by defining two terms that we use quite often.

Christian vocation—the word *vocation* means "calling," and every one of us is called by God to serve him. We are all called to serve God wherever we are, in whatever we do. This is the Protestant understanding of Christian vocation. God calls all of us to serve him where we are.

But there is another term:

Church-related vocation—which means that some are called to carry on the varied professional ministries of the church. It appears that the minister receives one call to be a Christian and another to be a Christian minister.

Some years ago, when I first came out of seminary, my bishop (Bishop Ellis Finger) asked me, as a newly ordained minister, to speak to the annual conference about my call to the ministry.

My initial response was very negative. "Why me? Of all people, why me?" There were so many ministers there who could have given a much more dramatic, spectacular, exciting, and inspiring testimony than I ever could have.

Not only that, but I also knew that when people think of the call to the ministry they think of highly dramatic, even miraculous happenings like Moses before the burning bush, Paul blinded on the Damascus Road, Luther caught in a thunderstorm, and Wesley being saved from a burning house.

But then I realized, if this is true, if this is the way people picture the call, then maybe that was all the more reason why someone like me should tell his story.

For God didn't call me through a burning bush. He didn't blind me. He didn't call me in a storm nor rescue me from a burning house.

Please don't misunderstand me. I am not disparaging dramatic calls. I am only saying that we can't limit God to acting only in that way.

My call to the ministry took a gradual and unspectacular form. It was and is a growing call.

Where did it take place?

It came in the church, and through the church!

God spoke to me not just on one Sunday, but over many Sundays. He spoke to me not just through one experience, but through many experiences. He spoke to me not just through one person, but through many: a church school teacher, a youth counselor, an encouraging friend, a member of my family, an interested pastor, and one very unlikely person.

Her name was Marie. She was a town character who wore high-top tennis shoes and a long red coat that was always buttoned to her chin year-round. She was very unusual, a strange personality, an "Apple Mary" type, and a devoted member of our church. She was a most unlikely person for God to speak through, and yet God spoke to me through her in this way.

I was in the tenth grade when suddenly one day after

church Miss Marie approached me. It startled me a bit because I was a little afraid of her. She was a strange-looking character.

"You don't know it yet," she said to me, "but God's gonna make a preacher out of you!"

That haunted me for two years. I wondered why she would say something like that. I thought about it. Was she right? Could that be possible? I honestly didn't know. I prayed about it. I tested God. I asked for a sign, a visible sign. For two years, I prayed and prayed and asked God over and over for some clue, for some dramatic sign, and got nothing. I asked for lightning in the sky and got nothing. I asked for a sign in the clouds. Nothing! I asked for it to rain. Nothing! I asked for it to stop raining. It rained harder!

Then, it dawned on me that the fact that I kept asking, the fact that I wanted the call so much was God's way of calling me. I was looking out there somewhere, and God was calling me within all along.

The Apostle Paul once said, "My call is from God, not men" (Galatians 1:1, paraphrased).

I would say: "My call is from God and not from men, but the church (along with a very unlikely character named Marie) was my hearing aid!"

Let me add two quick comments here:

First, to young people, let me just say that God is calling you to serve him and he may well be calling you to the ministry.

Second, to the church, my personal experience suggests something very important to us. We in the church should work at creating the warm kind of atmosphere whereby people can hear the voice of God.

BE QUICK TO LISTEN, SLOW TO SPEAK, AND SLOW TO ANGER

P lease, won't somebody listen to me!" Those were the words on a note found beside the unconscious girl.

She had taken an overdose of sleeping pills. An ambulance rushed her to the hospital where her stomach was pumped. When the girl awoke in the emergency room, doctors and nurses were standing over her, trying to talk to her. Suddenly, she screamed at them, "Talk, talk, talk. Everybody always talks! Won't anybody listen?"

In her frustration, the girl had dramatically underscored a key problem in life—most people talk much more than they listen. Even when they give the appearance of listening, they are not always hearing what is said. Listening is not easy, but without question it is one of the supreme acts of love. Reuel Howe, in his book *Creative Years*, calls listening "the first work of love."

Have you ever noticed how much the Bible says about listening? The word *listen* is used over 185 times. The word *hear* is used 450 times and other forms of those words are found 600 times in the Bible. That's a total of 1,200 times. The Scripture writers must have thought listening was important!

One of those references is found in James 1:19: "Let everyone be quick to listen, slow to speak, slow to anger." Think of that: quick to listen, slow to speak, and slow to anger.

Listening. There is no higher honor one person can pay another than to listen, to try to understand. It says, "You are real, you are valued, you matter, you are important to me, you are cared about, you are loved."

With this in mind, let me outline some things we need to remember if we are to become good listeners.

First, remember that there is a real difference between listening and lecturing. Sometimes we don't hear what is being said to us because we are too busy getting up a lecture.

Why do we think we have to lecture? Why do we think we have to preach to people? Why do we think we have to give advice? Most people don't want advice.

They want someone to listen, hear, care, and understand. They don't want a lecture. They want love! We need to be leery of lecturing people. As Benjamin Franklin supposedly said, "Don't give advice. Wise folks don't need it! Fools won't heed it!"

Second, remember that there is a real difference between listening and bustling. Some of us get so caught up in the hectic pace of life that we miss real life. The bustle, the busyness, the pressures so mesmerize us that we tune out and just cope through the days. Then joy, feeling, and listening get lost in the shuffle.

Third, remember that there is a real difference between listening and lamenting. The lamenter is the down-in-the-mouth listener, the woe-is-me listener who only hears the bad and then makes everyone around miserable. The lamenter is the pessimistic listener who is bound and determined, no matter what you say, to make something bad come out of it and to use it against you.

Fourth, remember that there is a real difference between listening and waiting your turn to speak. The Scriptures tell us to be quick to listen and slow to speak, but we forget that. Often, when we are supposed to be listening, we are not listening at all because we're thinking ahead about what we are going to say.

That's why we have trouble catching people's names when we first meet them; we are not listening to them. We are waiting our turn to speak.

Fifth, remember that there is a real difference between listening and reacting.

Remember that last part of the scripture verse: "Slow to anger." "Be quick to listen, slow to speak, and slow to anger."

Have you ever tried to talk to someone who always reacts? No matter what you say, they react in an angry or hostile tone.

You can't have much communication that way. Usually the reactor takes over and controls, and the other person's spirit eventually is broken. Then communication stops altogether. When communication stops, you're in big trouble.

Where there is no communication, there is no relationship. It's that simple.

Don't be a reactor. Don't be hostile. It kills communication. It hurts those you love. Remember how Abraham Maslow put it: "If the only tool you have is a hammer, you tend to treat everything as if it were a nail."

So, be quick to listen, slow to speak, and slow to anger. God gave us two eyes, two ears, and one mouth. There's a sermon there. Maybe we ought to do a lot less talking—and more seeing and listening.

CELEBRATING YOUR OWN UNIQUENESS AND THE UNIQUENESS OF OTHERS

Every person is a unique child of God. We must not miss this. We dare not take that uniqueness away. The loving human being understands that, sees that, embraces that, and celebrates that!

The Bible speaks of our uniqueness as our special gift from God. "Some would be apostles, some prophets, some evangelists, some pastors and teachers" (Ephesians 4:11). "The body does not consist of one member but of many" (1 Corinthians 12:14). And all the members are needful, all are helpful. God must have loved variety. He made so much of it.

As individuals, we must not be satisfied with merely becoming like everybody else.

Also, we must avoid forcing our way on everybody else.

We are different.

Some are tall and some are short; some like Bach and some like Willie Nelson; some love opera and some love football.

We have different temperaments, interests, opinions, and gifts, and that's OK. Indeed, it is beautiful—as long as we are loving, kind, tolerant, and understanding about it.

But, here is the rub. If we are insecure, then we tend to see everyone different from us as a threat to us. When that happens, we become scared and panicky and we react by trying to force our way on them. We want to make other people be like us. We want to make them do things our way. We feel compelled to prove that our way is the right way, the valid way, the only way. And we may think those people who see things differently are cruel, stupid, or insensitive. So we choose sides.

That is precisely what had happened in the Corinthian Church, and that is why Paul had to write to them to straighten them out.

When Paul wrote to the Christians in Corinth, they were in big trouble. Their church was torn apart by their differences. They had chosen sides and split into factions. There was misunderstanding and there was suspicion. There was blatant immorality. There were lawsuits among the church members. There were arguments, accusations, in-fighting, and struggles for power and position.

Their differences were killing them spiritually. So Paul wrote to them and in essence he said, "It's OK to be different! Your uniqueness is God's gift to you, and the loving person is the one who sees that and embraces that. If only we could learn how to disagree without being disagreeable. If only we could learn to celebrate our own uniqueness and the uniqueness of others! And the key to doing that is love."

Look at how Paul develops that in 1 Corinthians. In the first eleven chapters, he exposes their sins and outlines their problems. Then, in chapter 12, he shows them that it's OK to be different.

Some have this gift and some have that gift.

Some have this talent and some have another talent.

Some can do this and some can do that.

We are different, but God made us that way. He made each of us to be unique and he can blend our differences and use them for good.

So stop squabbling over who is right and who is wrong. Stop quarreling over whose way is best because now I want to show you a better way, a more excellent way, the best way of all—the way of *love*!

And then Paul gives us some of the most dramatic words in all of Scripture, the love chapter, 1 Corinthians 13, which ends with these powerful words: "And now faith, hope, and love abide, these three; and the greatest of these is love" (v. 13).

THE AHS AND BLAHS
OF LIFE

Life for all of us is a mixture of moods and experiences. Life is no smooth railroad trip across level plains, but rather it's more like a roller coaster ride with breathless ups and downs, with the ahs of the mountaintop and the blahs of the valley.

We can remember those high moments of joy when life feels good and really worth the living. However, we also know those low moments of depression and discouragement when we feel hopeless and are ready to throw in the towel and give up on life. We have all experienced both the ahs and blahs of life. We can all relate to the words of the spiritual, "Sometimes I'm up, sometimes I'm down. O, yes, Lord."

Speaking of the ups and downs and ahs and blahs; remember the Apostle Paul. If ever a human being had a life of mountains and valleys, joys and sorrows, challenges and threats, victories and tragedies, it was the Apostle Paul. He reports in one of his letters that he had experienced the debilitating experiences of life and the abounding experiences too.

He had faced plenty and hunger, abundance and want. He had incredible triumphs, but he also had troubles enough to dampen his spirit and break his soul. He could have so easily given in to the blahs. And then came the crowning blow. He was arrested and sent to prison. But from that prison cell, he wrote to his friends and said, "I have learned to be content with whatever I have. . . . I can do all things through him who strengthens me" (1 Corinthians 4:11, 13).

In the experience of Paul we see a powerful axiom of faith, namely, that God does not save us from trouble, but he does save us from fear and defeat! God is with us in the ups and downs, the ahs and blahs of life.

Now, how can we discover this contentment Paul had? More and more people fall victim to the blahs, this feeling of emptiness, drabness, depression, and boredom. For many, life has lost its zest and excitement and they have given in to a gray, dreary existence, a constant state of surrendered discontent. Then, too, all of us know those momentary lapses into blah moods. So the question is: How do we handle the blahs? What is the answer of faith? Here are some possible answers:

First, remember that it's temporary. Don't accept the blahs as permanent. Remember that this too will pass. Momentarily, you may be under a cloud, but behind the cloud the sun is still shining and soon the cloud will move on and you will be out in the clear again.

Second, make high use of low moments. Low moments will come to all of us, but we don't have to be defeated by them. We can use them, convert them, redeem them, and turn them into victories. That's what Paul did. It was a low moment when he was put in a prison cell. He could have resented that. He could have given in to bitterness. He could have cursed the darkness. Or he could have accepted it stoically and said, "Oh, well, I've done my part." But no! There in prison he sat down and wrote words that will live forever, letters now included in the New Testament. He used his low moments for high purposes and we can do that, too.

Third, learn to see the "ah" of things. The ah moments are all around us. They are as near as breathing, if only we could open our eyes to see them. There are so many things in life that are so beautiful, so wondrous, that words cannot describe them. We can only say ah in admiration. Nothing will help us handle the blahs more creatively than sensing the ah of God's presence and goodness and majesty.

Fourth, attack the blahs with a positive faith. Again, remember how Paul put it: "I can do all things through him who strengthens me" (Philippians 4:13). That's positive, isn't it?

Fifth, remember that there is an outside source of strength. When the blahs come, they make us feel so all alone. But the good news of faith is that we are not alone. God is with us. He will not desert us. He will not forsake us. He will be with us and he will see us through. Remembering that can make all the difference.

TRAVEL LIGHT

If you were leaving on a trip tomorrow morning, you would pull out the suitcases tonight and begin to pack. And there would be certain things that you would need to take along for the trip to be most comfortable and meaningful.

I read recently of a young bride who went on her honeymoon to the mountains with no shoes but the high heels she had on when she left the wedding. She left in such a hurry that she forgot her shoes!

A couple of years ago, I was privileged to go on a trip to the Holy Land. When we left, it was warm in Texas. I knew also that it would be warm in Jerusalem and Bethlehem and Cairo, so I didn't take an overcoat. But, there was one thing I didn't count on. We had to change planes in New York, where it was ten degrees below zero and snowing. We stood outside in the frigid elements for thirty minutes waiting for a bus to take us to our departure terminal. Over and over (as I stood there without a coat) I said through chattering teeth to concerned friends, "Oh, no! I'm not cold!" I did learn something though. It's hard to sound macho when your teeth are chattering!

That was one time I didn't take enough, but my problem is usually the reverse. I usually take too much. I think it is probably because I don't plan ahead. I run in at the last minute and start grabbing things to take along with very little forethought or planning.

Now, that brings us to one of the central faith problems of our time, specifically, what to take along on our life's journey.

Don't we have trouble in trying to decide what to take along and what to leave behind? What to carry and what to unload? What is essential and what is excess baggage? Some of the great minds of history have wrestled with this problem—and all have come to the same conclusion: that we need to travel light.

Remember how Thoreau put it: "Simplify! Don't fritter away your life on nonessentials!"

Remember how William Barclay said it when he was in his eighties: "I am an old man. I have lived a long time and over the years I have learned that in life there are very few things that really matter, but those few things matter intensely!"

Remember how Jesus put it: "Do not be so anxious. But seek first the kingdom of God and his righteousness and everything else falls in place!" (Matthew 6:31, 33, paraphrased).

Now, each of these is really saying the same thing: travel light! Decide early on what is important to you, what really matters to you, and give your energies to those things. We can't take everything with us on this life journey so we have to choose. We have to decide what is essential and weed out all the rest.

Well, the question is then: What do we pack? What do we include in our baggage? What do we take along?

Let me suggest three things, three principles that we all need to take with us down the road.

First, we need a sense of God's supportive presence over us, the blessed assurance that he is with us and watching over us.

Second, we need a sense of God's challenge, the constant challenge to grow, to be better, to do better, to try harder, to hunger and thirst for righteousness.

Third, we need a sense of God's ultimate victory for us—the confidence that nothing, not even death, can separate us from God and his love.

As you travel, travel light, but be sure to take these three things along.

THE POWER OF LOVE

It was Friday night. We were sitting in Caddo Parish Stadium in Shreveport, Louisiana, doing what we had done many times before, watching our son, Jeff, play football for the Captain Shreve Gators. He was playing the best game of his high school career when suddenly trouble struck, and a pleasant evening at the football game turned into a nightmare.

Jeff was down, writhing in pain, holding his right knee. Through the field glasses, we could see his face. He was in anguish.

Only moments before, we had been so happy. He had scored a touchdown on a fifty-yard pass play. But the play was called back because the referee had called a penalty.

Jeff was playing flanker. He cut across the middle. The ball was thrown high and behind him. I didn't think

89

he had a chance to catch it, but somehow he went up high, twisted back, and came down with the ball. Just as the right leg was planted stiff into the ground, the hit came—directly at the knee.

Immediately, everyone in the stands knew both players were hurt. The safety for the Airline High team was knocked out momentarily, and Jeff had torn ligaments in his knee.

Jeff had made the catch and held on to the ball despite the severe pain. It was a first down and the Gators went on to score—and win. Jeff said later he "gave his body for the team."

He was carried off the field in excruciating pain. We placed him in the back of a pickup, where we tried, without much success, to keep his leg stable as we were rushed across the practice field to a waiting van and then on to the clinic and eventually to surgery.

The surgery was successful and the prognosis was good, but it would be a slow process: surgery, then three to four days of intense pain, then six weeks in a cast and six more weeks on crutches, and after that months of physical therapy.

When something like that happens, so many "if onlys" flood into your mind.

If only the pass hadn't thrown Jeff off balance.

If only the right foot had been an inch off the ground.

If only the tackle had been a fraction higher, it never would have happened.

But it did happen, and Jeff was compelled to live with that fact. He was compelled to deal with this difficult situation. He didn't want to be out for the rest of that season but was compelled to be. He didn't want to be incapacitated for months but was compelled to be. He didn't want to be unable to drive a car for months but was compelled to be.

Now, when things like this are thrust upon us and we are compelled to face them, we have a choice: We can become bitter and cynical or we can rise above it, learn from it, and grow from it.

Jesus gives an illustration of this in the Sermon on the Mount when he says: "whoever compels you to go one mile, go with him two" (NKJV).

The key word here is *compel*. The people of Palestine were an occupied country, a slave state to Rome.

Roman soldiers were all about, with their flashy uniforms, swaggering attitudes, and sharp spears. They could at any moment "compel" any citizen of the occupied country to supply food, to run errands, to carry baggage, and sometimes the soldiers exercised this right of compulsion in the most tyrannical ways.

Always this threat of being compelled to do something undesirable hung over the occupied people. So I'm sure that Jesus' command to go the second mile was hard to swallow and difficult for them to accept.

Yet Jesus is underscoring here a very important truth, expressly, don't give in to bitterness or resentment or vengeance or retaliation. Rather, in every circumstance, even when compelled to deal with a difficult problem, rise above it and respond with love and courage and serenity and confidence.

GOD IS WITH US . . . ALWAYS

At the very end of his book *The Morning after Death*, Dr. L. D. Johnston tells the poignant and moving story of a nineteenth-century Congregational minister of New England. His name was John Todd.

He had been left an orphan when he was six. He was a frightened and confused little boy. But a beloved favorite aunt rose to the occasion and took him in and loved him as if her were her own child.

She saw to his every need and supported him in every way. She enabled him to complete his early schooling and to finish Yale College and to go on to seminary. She beamed proudly when he became an ordained minister.

Sometime later, when John Todd was pastor at Pittsfield, Massachusetts, he received one morning a tender letter from his then-aged aunt. She told him that she was in great distress and terribly frightened. The doctor had told her that she had a terminal illness. He had informed her that she was the victim of an incurable disease and that she would die very soon.

So, she wrote John, her nephew. He had been to college and seminary; he had read books and was very wise. She wrote asking the hard questions which were, as never before, weighing on her mind and burdening her soul. Could John reassure her? Could John tell her about death? Was there anything to fear?

This was John Todd's wise answer:

> It is not thirty-five years since I, a little boy of six, was left quite alone in the world. You sent we word that you would give me a home and be a kind mother to me.
>
> I have never forgotten that day when I made the long journey of ten miles from my home in Killingsworth to your home in North Killingsworth. I can still recall my uncertainty and disappointment when I learned that instead of coming for me yourself, you sent your man-servant Caesar to fetch me. I can still remember my tears and my anxiety as, perched on your horse and clinging tight to Caesar, I started for my new home.

Then John Todd went on to describe his childish anxiety as darkness fell before the journey was ended and how he wondered if his aunt would have gone to bed before he got there. They had ridden out of the woods into a clearing and, sure enough, there was a friendly candle in the window, and his aunt was waiting and watching at the door.

He remembered her warm arms gently lifting him, a tired and bewildered little boy, down from the horse. She had given him supper beside the bright fire in her hearth and then taken him to his room and sat beside him till he dropped off to sleep. "You are probably wondering why I am now recalling all these things to your mind," he added.

"Well, someday soon God will send for you to take you to a new home. Don't fear the summons. Don't fear the strange journey. Don't fear the messenger of death. At the end of the road you will find love and a welcome; you will be safe in God's care and keeping. God can be trusted, trusted to be as kind to you as you were to me so many years ago."

This wonderful story reminds us of God's most significant promise, namely, that he is with us! He will not desert us or forsake us. He will always be there for us.

Nothing—not even death—can separate us from him!

That is the good news of our faith. We don't have to be afraid because God can be trusted.

WE ARE GOD'S FAMILY

A great deal of life is like looking for your glasses when you already have them on. So it is with the biblical teachings about God and about people and about us.

Over and over and over again, the Bible reminds us that God is our Father and that we are his family. We are brothers and sisters, but we overlook this or forget it or neglect it or ignore it.

Jesus made it clear. He reminds us that our father in heaven loves all of his children and that God wants us to live daily in that caring, loving spirit. He reminds us that we have one Father—the one in heaven.

Now, the logic of this is inescapable.

There is one God who is the Father of us all.

If God is the Father of us all, then humanity is a family.

If humanity is a family, then all people are brothers and sisters.

This is what the Bible has always told us. At this point we join hands with all people everywhere. We are family! We are in this together. God is our Father and we are his children.

This is the message of the Ten Commandments. Remember how Jesus summed them up:

Love God and love people.

Love God and love your neighbor.

Love God, your Father in heaven, and your brothers and sisters beside you.

Look with me for a moment at the Ten Commandments. I am convinced that within these Ten Commandments are the positive principles through which God can work in us to bring about a deeper understanding of others and a more genuine love and appreciation of others.

Elton Trueblood, in his book *Foundations for Reconstruction*, has turned the Ten Commandments around. He has taken them out of the negative form and instead reveals their positive principles poetically. Thus in the Ten Commandments, we see not just a list of negative taboos, but rather a positive, emphatic call for love and loyalty to God, and love and loyalty to one another.

It's interesting to note here that the first, second, and third commandments call for love and devotion to God (put God first, worship God alone, be faithful to God's name).

The fourth commandment calls for love and devotion to the church (serve God through his church, remember the holy day of the Lord).

The fifth and seventh commandments call for love and devotion to the family (honor your parents, establish godly homes, be faithful to the church in your house, be faithful to your chosen mate).

Now, the remaining four commandments, the sixth, eighth, ninth, and tenth commandments, call for love and devotion to other people (remember the sacredness and integrity of people, remember that we are all children who share the same heavenly Father, the same Creator and Redeemer). Remember that we are brothers and sisters and that we are meant to love one another.

WE HAVE MET THE ENEMY AND HE IS US

In a *Pogo* comic strip some years ago, Pogo was on target when he said: "We have met the enemy and he is us!" The great educator Williams James would have agreed with that. He once said that at least 85 percent of our suffering is self-induced. We bring most of our suffering upon ourselves. Physically, it's true. Emotionally, socially, mentally, and spiritually, it's true.

There is a graphic line in *The Diary of Anne Frank* that speaks to this. Maybe you recall the scene. Anne Frank and eight other Jewish people had been hiding out from the Nazis for many months. Suddenly, the pressure of confinement and living so close together caused a serious argument. The long-repressed resentments burst into the open in a very bitter exchange. Then Anne's father said:

"If we continue the way we are going, the Nazis will not have to destroy us. We will have destroyed ourselves."

Now that's a timely warning for all of us, a warning we need to take seriously. The real issues of life more often than not are decided within us—not out there. It is not the external pressures that undo us. It's trouble within. Someone said it well. "The ruination of most people is themselves."

Shakespeare knew this, and he built his tragedies around this insight. No tragedies in literature can compare to his, and one of the reasons for his greatness is that he saw that life's real tragedy lurks within ourselves.

The old Greek dramatists, as they wrote their plays, caused their victims to suffer tragedy because of mysterious comic fate or because of some whim of the gods. But Shakespeare shifted the battlefield to the souls of people—people like you and me. Cassius says in *Julius Caesar*, "The fault, dear Brutus, is not in our stars. / But in ourselves."

Hamlet wrestles with hesitant indecision; Macbeth wrestles with ambition and remorse; Othello wrestles with insatiable jealousy.

You see, the greatest characters in Shakespeare's tragedies are all having it out with their own souls, and most often the trouble was of their own making.

The truth is that much of the trouble we have to face is not that formidable in and of itself. We are really more often tripped up by our fears. And sadly, the fear of trouble can be more crushing than the trouble itself. Persons seldom work themselves into a nervous breakdown; they worry themselves into it.

Just think of the list of phobias, which have been multiplied in our age of anxiety, and notice how many of them are what Archibald MacLeish called "faceless fears." They include fear of the dark, fear of open places, fear of closed places, fear of heights, fear of the future, fear of old age, fear of death, all the way to phobophobia, which is fear of fear itself. There are seventy-two listed phobias, most of them shadows with no power to hurt except through the way the fear undoes us.

And this is where faith comes in. Nothing enables us to overcome fear so much as an awareness deep within that God is with us, that he will see us through, that he loves us and will not desert us or forsake us. This is what the psalmist is talking about when he says, "I will fear no evil: for thou art with me" (Psalm 23:4 KJV). This is what Jesus is talking about when he says over and over, "Fear not! Fret not! Don't be anxious! Don't be afraid." This is what Paul is talking about when he says, "I can do all things through him who strengthens me" (1 Corinthians 4:13).

When life is undergirded by faith and a sense of God's love and presence, we are released from the "faceless fears," and we are better able to manage and handle our troubles. This confidence that God is with us is a "Bridge over Troubled Waters." Someone has wisely pointed out that in the Scriptures, there are 365 "fear nots." That's one for every day of the year!

USE IT OR LOSE IT

One of the most perplexing verses in the Bible is Matthew 25:29, which says, "For to all those who have, more will be given, and they will have an abundance; but from those who have nothing, even what they have will be taken away."

What can this mean? Why give more to a person who has plenty and take away from a person who has so little? It sounds so unfair, and for that reason the verse is a frustrating mystery to many people.

To unravel the mystery, it helps, of course, to see the verse in context. It comes at the end of Jesus' Parable of the Talents.

Remember the parable with me. A man going on a journey left five talents with one servant, two talents with another servant, and one talent with still another servant. Then he went away.

During his absence the servant with five talents traded with his and made five more. The servant with two talents used his to earn two more. But the servant with one talent buried his in the ground for safe keeping because he was afraid. He was afraid of his master, afraid of failure, afraid to take a risk, afraid to try. Paralyzed by his fear, he did nothing. He buried his talent in the ground.

When the master returned, he commended the two servants who had used their gifts and increased them. But when the one-talent servant came in for the accounting, the master became quite upset with him because he had done nothing. The master rebuked him, called him "wicked" and "lazy." But more than that, he took away the servant's one talent and gave it to the servant with ten talents. Then comes that haunting verse.

"For to all those who have, more will be given, and they will have an abundance; but from those who have nothing, even what they have will be taken away."

Now, what is this all about? The key that unlocks this is to understand that the true meaning stands out when we see that Jesus is not talking about money here. He is not talking about bank stocks or real estate. He is talking about our abilities and our inner determination to use what we have.

Here, Jesus is underscoring a fascinating and dependable principle of life. If we don't use our gifts and talents, we lose them. If we don't use our abilities, they shrivel and die.

The truth of that principle is as wide as life itself. Ask any athlete or musician. Ask any artist or scholar. Ask any salesman or surgeon. Ask any writer or preacher. Each in his or her own way will tell you that he or she has learned from experience that this is true.

"We either use our talents or we lose them!"

This principle literally pervades every area of life. Let me show you what I mean.

First, it's true on the physical level. We all know our physical talents and capabilities are enhanced, improved, and increased by use, exercise, and practice. This is what gives the sailor his keen eye, the pianist his nimble wrist, the surgeon her deft hand, the runner her grace and endurance. When we use our physical talents, we increase them. If we don't use them, we lose them.

Second, it's true on the intellectual level. If we stretch our minds, they grow, but if we put our minds into neutral and stop learning, our minds shrivel up on us. They wither and die.

Third, it's true on the social level. The cloistered life doesn't work. The hermit life doesn't work because we are relational people. God made us social beings. He meant for us to live together in relationships as his family. When we cut people out of our lives, we suffer. We become frightened, anxious, and sometimes even paranoid.

Fourth, it's true also on the spiritual level. If practice makes perfect in music, golf, art, poetry, or speaking, then it must be true that practice enhances the spiritual graces.

If you want to have a good prayer life, how do you do it? You pray a whole lot.

If you want to have a good grasp of Scripture, how do you do it? You study the Scriptures—and study and study some more.

If you want to be a good churchgoer, how do you do it? You get in church. You participate. You live it, learn it, work at it.

When it comes to faith, that's the choice open to us. We use it or lose it.

WHY DO WE WAIT FOR PERMISSION?

Have you ever noticed that many people go through life waiting for permission to really live?

Indeed, many people are frustrated because they have never really outgrown the security of being controlled by someone else. They don't feel that they have permission to take charge of their own lives so they wait around for someone else out there to give them permission.

In Luke 13, we see a vivid example of this. Jesus sees a woman in the synagogue who has been bent double by some spiritual burden. She has been unable to stand up straight for over eighteen years.

Jesus has compassion for her, and he gives her permission to put the problem behind her.

"Woman, you are set free from your ailment," he said to her (v. 12). And she straightened up and praised God.

That's wonderful, but why did she have to wait eighteen years? Why didn't someone give her permission earlier to throw off this burden? Why didn't she give herself permission? Why did she resign herself to this awful plight? And why do we? Why do we wait around for permission?

That woman was "bent over" by a "spirit" that had gripped her and shackled her for almost twenty years (v. 11). For all that time she had not been able to stand up straight because she was so ashamed, so guilt-ridden, so worn down, so burdened, so humiliated.

Then Jesus happened along and, perceptive as he was, he saw straight to the core of her problem. He told her to put it behind her. In effect, he gave her permission to straighten up, and she did!

Don't miss something very important in this story, that her problem was a spiritual one. You remember, of course, that in many of the healing miracles in Jesus' ministry, the focus is on something physical—blindness, lameness, or illness—a physical disease or disability.

In this story, though, the woman is bent double because of something gone wrong spiritually.

Don't you wish we could know the rest of the story? Don't you wish the writer had given us a bit more information, a few more details?

Had she been involved in some public scandal that had left her stooped in shame?

Had she been caught in some sordid sin that had left her doubled over in humiliation?

Had she done something so terrible that people steered clear of her for fear of guilt by association?

Had her past been so scarlet that it had burdened her to the point where she was bent down with guilt?

We just don't know. The Scriptures don't tell us. They only give us the bottom line, namely, that when Jesus said to her, "You are set free from your ailment" that was all she needed to unbend. When he assured her that she was forgiven, it set her free from the awful burden that had been pushing her down for so many years.

Jesus' permission miraculously made it feel all right to forgive herself, pick up the pieces of her life, and start all over again.

Isn't that a great story? It sounds (at first hearing) like an ancient story, far removed from where we live. But look closer and notice the "permission syndrome."

The woman was resigned to her plight until Jesus came along and gave her permission to be OK, permission to start over, permission to live again. Like her, we often wait around for permission to live. The good news of Christ is that he sets us free, unshackles us, relieves us of our burdens, forgives us, encourages us, and inspires us. That is, he gives us permission to live—to really live!

NOT TRYING IS WORSE
THAN TRYING AND FAILING

Let me begin with three quick stories. Look, if you will, for the common thread that runs through them.

The first story comes from the great British minister Leslie Weatherhead. When Dr. Weatherhead was a young man working his way through college, he took a job one summer as a door-to-door salesman. He had many memorable experiences that summer, but the one he remembered most vividly was one that saddened him greatly—the family who met him at the door and said coldly, "Son, you are wasting your time here 'cause we ain't interested in nothing!"

The second story tells of a man who waited all his life outside a door. He looks at the door and longs to enter it. He watches the doorkeeper and wonders how to get past him and through the door. For some time, he plots and strategizes ways to get through the door.

Afraid to try, finally he gives up—tired, disappointed, and disillusioned.

In the end, as the man is dying, he says to the door-keeper, "Why? Why did you keep me out?"

"I didn't," answers the doorkeeper. "As a matter of fact, this is your door and I am here to serve you."

"But why did you stand in my way?" asks the dying man. "Why did you block me?"

"I didn't," replied the doorman. "You never asked to come in."

The third story comes from history. Some years ago in South America, a crew of Peruvian sailors was cruising up the Amazon River when they came upon a strange sight. A Spanish ship was at anchor in the middle of the wide Amazon River, and all the crew members were ly-ing weakly on the deck of the ship.

As the Peruvian sailors drew closer, they saw that the Spanish sailors were in serious trouble. They were in ter-rible physical condition. They looked awful, like the pic-ture of death itself. Their lips were parched and swollen. The Spanish sailors were indeed dying of thirst.

"Can we help you?" shouted the Peruvians.

The Spaniards cried out, "Water! Water! We need freshwater!"

The Peruvian sailors, surprised at their request, told them to lower their buckets and help themselves.

The Spanish mariners had thought they were lost and doomed in the open ocean. They had thought the water around them was undrinkable. So they had given up hope. They had quit trying. They had dropped anchor and laid down to die.

They were dying of thirst when, as a matter of fact, they were a couple of miles up in the mouth of the freshwaters of the Amazon River. They had been anchored there for days. For days, they had been in the midst of freshwater and they didn't know it. They didn't discover it. Do you know why? Because they had given up and quit trying.

Now, of course, the thread that runs through these stories is the problem of quitting on life, giving up, and throwing in the towel. This defeated spirit is the opposite of commitment.

Apathy means quitting on life. It is the opposite of commitment.

We all dread the thought of failure. But worse than trying and then failing, is not trying at all.

The silent tragedy of life is that many people reach the point of death only to find that they never really lived, they never really loved, they never really tried.

SUCCESS, FAILURE: HOW DO YOU TELL THE DIFFERENCE?

For many years now, we in America have been highly success conscious or success oriented. Most have agreed with Webster's definition: success is the attainment of wealth and fame. Think about it. Isn't it true that when we think of success, we immediately pull out names like Rockefeller, Ford, DuPont, Trump? They symbolize the sweet smell of success!

But Webster was wrong. Money and fame are not enough. Those who have risen to the top of the heap are sometimes the most miserable. Their success is often a sham.

Recently, there was a cartoon in the *Saturday Review*. A portly, bewhiskered king is wearing a luxurious ermine robe and a magnificent jeweled crown. He is sitting in his money counting house. Coins are stacked high on the table. Sacks of money are all around his feet. He is trying to amuse himself by counting his money, but there is a bored, tired, weary look on his face. The queen stands nearby. She, too, wears her ermine robe and her costly crown. But both look frightfully unhappy as she says, "Well, I'm getting sick and tired of eating bread and honey and caviar, too!"

You see, there is more to successful living than eating well and counting wealth. Our customary standards of measuring success are so shoddy. "How much money do you make?" "How many cars do you have?" "When was the last time you had breakfast in Paris, my dear?" The very questions reflect our poverty of soul and our shallowness of understanding.

It's interesting to note that we get a vastly different understanding of what success is in the teachings of Jesus. His approach is so different that it startles us. In effect, he says: "Whoever wants to be first must be last of all and servant of all" (Mark 9:35). A servant! What on earth could Jesus mean by that? Successful people aren't servants; successful people have servants. What is he trying to do here—upset our whole scale of values? Yes! That is precisely what he is trying to do—to give us a whole new scale of values, a new set of standards for measuring success, specifically these:

First, success is not so much dependent on outer circumstances as it is on inner stability. Real success is not out there somewhere; it is within. The rich people who are happy are those who would be happy even if they were not rich. It is good to have money and the things money can buy, but real success is in having the things money cannot buy. How rare is this inner strength these days. People chain smoke, despite the consequences, because they are nervous within. People become habitual drinkers, despite the consequences, because they are restless within. People drug themselves or tranquilize themselves because the mounting pressures of life have torn their inner world to shreds. Some people would give anything for a good night's rest, for a sense of peace within. Inner strength is the only success that really matters.

Second, success is not so much having many possessions as it is pursuing a dream. Real success lies in giving your life to and for something bigger than you are: a dream, a cause, a purpose, a ministry. That is more important than all the money and all the material possessions in the world.

Third, success is not living for self; it is living for others. Remember the little boy who studied the Parable of the Good Samaritan and was then asked what he learned. He said, "I learned that when I'm in trouble, somebody ought to help me." He missed the whole point—and so often so do we. By present-day standards of success, Jesus wouldn't measure up so well. Born in a stable. His mother was a peasant girl; his father a carpenter. Had little formal schooling, wrote no books, held no offices, no political fame, traveled very little. He taught, but many scoffed at his teaching. His closest friends betrayed him. And then, almost before the story got good and started, he was nailed to a cross like a common criminal.

That doesn't sound like a success story, does it? And yet, 2,000 years later, people bow at his name and look in amazement at his perceptive teaching. People's lives are changed because of him. Why? Because he showed us what God is like and what God wants us to be like—and the word is *love*! He who is greatest and most successful among you, let him be a servant—a servant of God, of people, of love.

TURNING PROBLEMS
INTO OPPORTUNITIES

D r. John Claypool once told of a strange idea he had as a little boy. He thought that he could outrun germs!

Once as a little boy, he came down with a terrible cold, and somehow he got the idea that if he could run fast from one room to another, he could get away from his germs the way he could get away from his pet puppy.

His mother found him dashing from room to room—all out of breath—and when she discovered what he was attempting to do, she gently, but wisely, called him back to reality.

She explained that he couldn't outrun the germs. No matter where or how fast he went, the germs would go with him. "The sooner you quit trying to run away from sickness," she said, "and start taking medicine for it, the quicker you will get well."

There is a great truth here, not only for treating colds but also for dealing with all of life's problems. And yet, we are so slow to learn that!

We can't outrun our problems. The sooner we accept this fact and decide to face them, the better. And yet we are so slow to understand that.

This incessant search for a way to escape the inescapable and the chronic resentment of problems are an incredible waste of energy. And yet (if we are honest) we must confess that we have squandered a large portion of our lives running, hiding, fleeing, escaping.

But, let me tell you something—problems are here to stay! There are no problem-free jobs. There are no problem-free marriages. There are no problem-free churches. There are no problem-free communities.

So we can't really run away. There is no escape. We have to face problems, deal with troubles, and handle difficulties. There is no hiding place, no place to run.

The only creative answer is to learn how to cope with our hardships productively.

Once again, our great teacher is Jesus. We see in him the model and pattern for dealing with problems meaningfully. In him, we see how to cope with difficulties in creative ways.

For example, remember the time when he fed 5,000 people in the wilderness. This famous story depicts Jesus up against a real down-to-earth problem—and the way he responded is fascinating.

First, notice that he chose to cope rather than to run. He chose to face the problem rather than flee. He refused to follow the disciples' suggestion that they employ the strategy of escapism. He decided to face the situation squarely and openly—trusting God to help him through it. Instead of saying, "Trouble is coming; let's go our way and let them go theirs," he said in effect, "We are involved in this event together. We cannot pass the buck. Let's face it and deal with it and do something about it."

And, with the help of God, he fed the thousands. It is clear from this response that for Jesus the way out was always the way through.

Second, Jesus surveyed the available resources. Sometimes we fail to do this. The problem looms so large and so formidable that we suffer from tunnel vision, from narrow vision, and as a result we are blinded to the available resources.

Third, when he trusted God and used what he had the best he could, the little became enough. Five loaves and two fishes were not much, but he used it in faith and God made it sufficient.

Fourth, with God's help, he turned the problem into an opportunity. Jesus was a master at that, wasn't he? He knew how to turn interruptions and difficulties and problems into opportunities. He knew how to turn bad things into good things. He knew how to turn defeats into victories. And with his help we can do that too! With his help, we can cope!

CLOWNS AND PROPHETS

Clowns and prophets have one thing in common; even as they speak the truth people laugh at both of them.

One of America's favorite clowns, columnist Erma Bombeck, once asked wives and mothers for specific suggestions on ways to prevent or terminate wars. Here are some of the suggestions that poured in to *The (Toledo) Blade* in 1981:

> Put the war in the hands of the post office. It might not stop it, but it would certainly slow it down.
> Assign children to war zones and tell them they have to clean their rooms before they can go.
> Tell your husband it's something he has to dress up for.

Transport troops via Amtrak.
Have one-size-fits-all uniforms that are issued
in little eggs.

But Bombeck's favorite solution came from a woman named Barb. Her son, on leave from the Marine Corps, hadn't been in the house five minutes before he and his fifteen-year-old brother got into a "knock-down-drag-out fight."

Barb reacted the way she had numerous times before: she grabbed a large wooden spoon, jumped between them, and gave them "the look." They knew better than to continue, so they separated and backed off. "Barb figured that the only way to end war is to draft experienced mothers, arm them with wooden spoons and 'the look,' and send them into battle."

Ridiculous you say? Erma concluded, "Not half as ridiculous as wars."

The clown speaks. She is laughed at. But does anybody hear?

The prophet speaks, too. He cries: "We are all God's family. We are brothers and sisters: No one is an island. Study war no more. Love your enemies. Pray for them. See other nations as neighbors, not as adversaries. Turn the other cheek. Forgive, love, be merciful. Set before you is life and death, blessing and curse; therefore choose life, that you and your children may live. Be peacemakers."

The prophet speaks, but is he laughed at? Is he taken seriously? Does anybody hear?

When will we ever learn? When will we ever see how ridiculous and how terrible war is?

Every now and then we have to be reminded. Every now and then we have to be jolted into the reality of how horrible and how destructive war can be.

That is what Yom HaShoah is about. It means "Day of (remembrance of) the Holocaust and the Heroism." It is the time in the spring each year when Jews and Christians join hands to remember with tears the horrors of war, the horrors of the Holocaust, and to remember with love the millions of victims whose lives were so brutally snuffed out.

When we look at the Holocaust and see so graphically the terrible consequences of bigotry and hatred and war, we are overwhelmed with the enormity of what happened. Our immediate reaction is to try to forget, to run from the pain, to wall off the memories. We want to hide the bones from sight, to whitewash the sepulchers.

Yet, as Henri Nouwen tells us in his book *The Living Reminder*, "to forget our sins may be an even greater sin than to commit them. Why? Because what is forgotten cannot be healed and that which cannot be healed easily becomes the cause of greater evil" (p. 17). What we forget may rear its head again and seize us by the throat before we recognize its danger.

And so, we remember. Painful as it is, we remember in the hope that it will never ever happen again.

THE BATTLE WITHIN

In the year 1900, a baby boy who was destined to become one of the great French writers was born in Lyon, France. His name was Antoine de Saint-Exupery.

He wrote beautifully and powerfully about nature and life, and he was the chief influence in the creating of the literature of aviation. He was a flyer himself.

During World War II, Saint-Exupery was called into active duty with the French Air Force. On July 31, 1944, during an unarmed observation mission, his plane was shot down by a young German flyer, and the great French writer was killed.

Now, it just so happened that the young German pilot who shot him down was an avid admirer of the French writer. When he learned who it was that he had shot down, he deeply regretted his actions and said that he would not have done it had he known who was in the other plane.

This story illustrates one of the great tragedies of life: that sometimes we unwittingly kill what we love—our marriages, our families, our friendships, our own selves, our relationship with God.

I once heard a young woman say to me through her tears, "Jim, I'm so ashamed. I don't know what gets into me, but sometimes I crucify people I love with cruel words. I destroy what I ought to value most!"

Now, blow that up a bit and you have the tragedy of Holy Week. Blow that up a bit and toss in some cloak-and-dagger tactics, some calculated cunning, some selfish scheming and you have the ingredients that produced Good Friday, Golgotha, the place of the skull, the crucifixion of Jesus.

Of course, it's easy enough to lay the blame on those who were in authority when Jesus was arrested and falsely accused and unfairly tried and brutally nailed to the cross.

It's easy enough to point the finger at Judas, at Pilate, at Herod, at Caiaphas.

It's easy enough to make them the scapegoats, but to do so may be to miss one of the key lessons of Jesus' life—that Jesus was put on the cross not so much by terribly evil, wicked people but by destructive, cancerous inner attitudes, destructive attitudes that still haunt us, which still wreck us, which still eat us up inside. These destructive attitudes within us can drag us to a level of life that is beneath what God meant us to have. And when that happens, someone may get crucified!

The people who put Jesus on the cross were not so much despicable people as they were people like you and me who lost control to despicable attitudes. They lost the battle within. And the fallout was that an innocent man suffered.

The inner life is so tremendously important, and that's where the most strategic battles are won and lost— inside!

The enemies within (like envy, jealousy, resentment, greed, hatred, selfishness)—these were the attitudes that nailed Jesus to the cross—and they still do!

Could it be that this is what the hymn writer had in mind when he wrote, "Were you there when they crucified my Lord?"

Well, every time we let one or more of these destructive attitudes take control of our lives, we are indeed then and there nailing Jesus—and all he stood for—to a cross.

Every time we give in to selfish, ruthless ambition or to jealousy or to hostility we are crucifying our Lord.

JESUS GIVES GOD A FACE

Some years ago, a woman died in New York City. And when the will was read, it was discovered that her number-one beneficiary was God. She had left a rather considerable estate simply "to God."

Isn't that a beautiful thought? She had remembered God in her will!

However, her act caused a long series of frustrating legal entanglements. In order to settle the estate properly, certain procedures were carefully followed.

A case was entered into court naming God as a party thereto. Legal summons was issued and the court went through the motions of trying to serve it.

The final report, however, to the court was eventually declared as follows: "After due and diligent search we have come to the conclusion that God cannot be found in New York City."

Well, I don't know about that, but I do know that God can be found dramatically, powerfully, and wonderfully in the Gospel of Luke.

Nowhere is the picture of God more beautifully painted than in the Gospel of Luke.

So much of what we know of God comes from Luke's pen. So much of what we prize about God comes from Luke as he shares with us so many unique things Jesus said and did that reflect his image of the Father.

This, for me, is the supreme truth of Christianity, namely, that in Jesus we see God.

When we see Jesus feeding the hungry, comforting the sorrowful, befriending the outcast, and helping the needy including the little children, then we can say, "This is what God is like!"

We need to see that and hear that, because the way we image God affects all that we say and do.

Remember the story about the little boy who was afraid of the dark and kept calling out to his mother. Trying to console him, his mother said to him, "You don't have to be afraid. God is there with you."

"I know that," answered the little boy, "but I want someone in here with me that's got a *face*!"

Well, you see that is the point, Jesus gives God a face, and the good news is that it's the face of love and concern and acceptance and compassion.

The key characteristic of the life and message of Jesus is that it is a gospel. The word *gospel* (*euangelion* in Greek) means "good news." It was good news that Jesus came to bring.

If, then, Jesus came to bring good news about God, it must mean that he came to tell people things about God that they did not know or did not realize before.

Before Jesus, people thought of God as unapproachable and unpredictable, as distant and detached, as austere and hidden, and as unfeeling and indifferent.

Before Jesus, people were afraid of God. Before Jesus, people thought God was hostile toward them. Before Jesus, people thought they were the victims of God, rather than the children of God.

But then came Jesus with his picture of the gracious, merciful, loving, forgiving Father God.

Nowhere is this picture seen more clearly than in Luke's Gospel. Nowhere is it depicted more graphically than in the Parable of the Prodigal Son.

When you think of God, what comes to your mind? I'll tell you what comes to my mind: the picture of that loving Father peering anxiously down the roadway day after day, month after month until he sees a familiar form returning home in the distant haze. Then, he leaves all dignity behind him and he rushes down the road to meet him and to embrace the disheveled, defeated, but much-loved prodigal son.

The picture of the loving, merciful, compassionate, forgiving Father—that's the way I picture him. Not angry or hostile or vengeful or cruel, but loving, caring, and forgiving.

WHAT IS THE SUBTLE DIFFERENCE?

It is significant to note that sometimes different people can experience the same events and yet be affected by those same events in radically different ways. Consider these examples.

Two young men have a father who is an alcoholic. One becomes an alcoholic. The other becomes a minister who works with alcoholics. Why? What is the subtle difference?

Two people receive the same bad news in the same situation. One is emotionally devastated, coming apart at the seams. The other becomes a tower of strength, an inspiration to everyone he meets. Why? What is the subtle difference?

In Tennessee a few years ago, two young men were jilted by their intended brides on the same day. One gave in to self-pity and jumped off a tall bridge trying to commit suicide. The other, just as brokenhearted, wrote out of his heartache a song that became a popular recording that brought him $300,000.

Why? What makes the difference? What is the subtle difference that affects persons so differently when they are experiencing an identical situation or an identical set of circumstances? Let me offer three quick observations:

First, the difference is the response. The subtle difference is how we respond, how we respond to adversity, how we respond to opportunity, how we respond to life. The key is to understand that what happens is not nearly so important as how we respond to what happens! The key thing is not the circumstances, not the events, but how we respond.

Second, the difference is not subtle; it is dramatic! It is the difference between defeat and victory, despair and hope, pessimism and optimism, sorrow and joy, death and life. The way you and I respond to things is the most important fact about our personal lives.

And third, the difference is between responding and reacting. I am using the word *respond* in a positive way and the word *react* in a negative way.

We react out of self-centered personal feelings. We respond out of self-giving concern for others. When I react, I'm thinking of my rights, my position, my place, my feelings, my interests. When I respond I'm thinking of others, of a cause, or more importantly of God.

Conversion is moving from reacting to responding! Conversion is moving from "that belongs to me" to "I belong to that."

General William Booth, founder of the Salvation Army, summed it up years ago when he was quoted as saying, "Damnation comes from mirrors, salvation from windows!"

DEALING WITH DISAPPOINTMENT CREATIVELY

Disappointment is a fact of living. As J. M. Barrie said, "Everyman's life is a diary in which he means to write one story and is forced to write yet another." Milton went blind; Beethoven lost his hearing; Pasteur became a paralytic at forty-six; Helen Keller was deaf, blind, and unable to speak; the Apostle Paul wanted to go to Spain with his work but instead got a prison cell in Rome.

But were they defeated by these disappointments? Absolutely not! They all, each and every one, turned their disappointments into the instruments of victory. We can do that, too! Indeed, this is our calling as people of faith, to turn defeats into victories.

How do we learn to suffer creatively like that? How do we turn our disappointments into instruments of victory? Here are a few practical suggestions:

Recognize that disappointments come to all people and that they are usually temporary; they pass, and life goes on.

Understand that you may rebel against them a bit. (I think that is probably all right for a while, because we cannot take life as apathetically as a pillow takes a punch.)

Beware of blaming others for your misfortune. Faith says to us that we don't need a scapegoat. We have a Savior! We are justified by God's grace, not by our victories.

Find a creative outlet for your pent-up energies. Talk it out or work it out constructively if you are physically able.

Go on with life, living one day at a time. (There are two days in each week about which we need not worry: yesterday and tomorrow.)

See your disappointment as a unique opportunity for serving God.

Trust God to be with you to sustain you and to open another door. Or, in other words, do your best and trust God with the rest!

THREE BREAKTHROUGHS
THAT CAN CHANGE
YOUR LIFE

Søren Kierkegaard, the great Danish theologian of another century, once told a parable about a wild duck who came to eat with the tame ducks in a farmer's barnyard.

The wild duck only meant to make a brief visit. He only meant to eat with the tame ducks in the barnyard for one day. But he enjoyed it so much that he decided to stay awhile.

Each day he ate more and more and, of course, grew heavier and heavier. He soon felt perfectly at home there on the ground in the barnyard.

When fall came and the wild ducks took to the skies and began flying overhead, something stirred within him. He decided it was time to move on. He longed to soar high into the skies.

But what do you think happened? He spread his wings to fly but there was no strength there. His body was too heavy, his wings were too weak. He could not get off the ground. He tried and tried, but he simply could not get over the fence. His lack of exercise and extra pounds had imprisoned him, so he soon gave up the idea and returned to the security of the barnyard.

The years passed. Each spring and fall, as the other wild ducks flew overhead he would look up and flap his wings, but then would settle back down to old, easy life. And it was not long before he did not even look up anymore.

Subtly and gradually, he had become a prisoner. Enslaved by his own lack of exercise, he forgot that he was meant for the skies!

Many people are like that: imprisoned in ruts of their own making.

The good news of faith is that we can be free. With the help of God, we can break out of those prisons that enslave and paralyze us.

The great freedom victories of life are won not on battlefields of military conflict, not in the sports arenas of the world, not in the marketplaces or in the scientific laboratories, not in the great expanses of space, but in the souls of people. The great battles of life are won and lost in the inner lives of people like you and me.

We find a remarkable account of three such victories recorded early in Paul's letter to the Philippian Christians. He loved them deeply. He wrote to them like a father writing to his children and he revealed in that magnificent letter three personal breakthroughs that can change your life. Here they are.

First, you don't have to be the victim of your circumstances. You and I can be victors rather than victims. Paul had made that personal breakthrough. He knew how to use his circumstances rather than to be enslaved by them. When Paul wrote to the Philippians, he was in prison, in ill health, facing death—pretty bad circumstances. But he refused to be victimized by his external situation. In those deplorable circumstances, he used the time not to feel sorry for himself but to write words that ultimately became treasured letters of the New Testament.

Second, you don't have to be a victim of your pride. Some of Paul's adversaries were using his imprisonment against him personally, saying that if he were God's man, he wouldn't be in prison. You might expect Paul to be angry or resentful or hurt. But no; look how he responds. He swallows his pride and says in effect, "So what? It doesn't matter what they say about me. All that matters is that the gospel is proclaimed."

It is really very simple: If we could be proud without being prideful, reverent without being pompous, committed without being closed-minded, pure without being holier-than-thou then our souls would be healthy and vibrant and free.

And third, you don't have to be afraid of death. Paul, like all great people of faith, was not afraid of death. He faced it squarely, confidently, and courageously. If life is Christ, then death will be more of Christ and it will not be death at all, but the entrance into a larger dimension of life with God. The great Christians have all been very sure of this. God is with us and for us and nothing (not even death) can separate us from him and his love. When you believe that, it sets you free!

ARE YOU EAGER
TO BE APATHETIC?

Do you remember the old Smothers Brothers routine in which Tom seems worried? Dick says, "What's the matter, Tom? You seem despondent."

"I am," replies Tom, "I'm worried about the state of the American society."

"Well, what bothers you? Are you worried about poverty in our nation?"

"No, that doesn't worry me."

"I see. Well, are you concerned about the danger of nuclear war?"

"No, that doesn't worry me."

"Are you upset about the use of narcotics among our youth?"

"No, that doesn't bother me."

"Well, then, if you're not bothered by poverty or war or drugs, what are you worried about?"

And Tom responds: "I'm worried about our apathy!"

Well, Tom Smothers, in his unique way, may have put his finger on one of the big problems of our time: apathy.

Apathy means quitting on life. And it is the opposite of faith and hope. It is the opposite of love and commitment.

To be apathetic (according to Roget's Thesaurus) is to be spiritless, heartless, and sluggish; it is to be numb, paralyzed, and insensitive. To be apathetic is to be unconcerned, unimpressed, unexcited, unmoved, unstirred, and untouched.

The noted author John Hersey wrote a bestseller entitled *Too Far to Walk*. It is a commentary on attitudes in our time. The title is drawn from an incident when a laid-back young man skips one of his college classes. When his friends ask why he missed class, he answers simply, "Aw, I got up this morning and I decided it was too far to walk." That is the not-very-pretty picture of apathy.

Now, we all dread the thought of failure. But worse than trying and then failing is not trying at all.

Apathy is not trying at all. It is absolutely refusing to get involved. And it is the worst failure!

If you try and fail, at least you know that you are alive, you are still in the game. But, not trying at all, not caring at all means that you have quit on life, that you have holed up in some kind of self-protective shell, and that you are numbered among the "walking dead."

The silent tragedy of life is that many people reach the point of death only to find that they never really lived; they never really loved; they never really tried; they never really got involved.

Somewhere along the way (and maybe even quite early), they got hurt or scared or disappointed and they quit; they refused to try anymore. Terrified by the risks and pressures and demands and hard decisions, they pulled back into their shells and hid and they became eager to be apathetic!

"Eager to be apathetic." It sounds like a contradiction, doesn't it? But that is exactly where so many people are these days.

Nothing is more humanly important than that we care; that we care about what's happening in the world or in the city or in our nation or in our schools and homes and churches; that we care about other people.

But the problems can become so complex and there are so many of them. Then we become confused and frightened even more by the media blitz: television, radio, newspapers, magazines, movies, the Internet. They bombard us with conflicting ideas.

And we get scared. We feel overwhelmed and cry, "What can one person do?" Many, many people bail out on life. They become eager to wash their hands of the whole mess. They become eager to be apathetic.

This is so tragic because apathy can be so dangerous!

Our apathy can cause people to get hurt.

Our apathy can cause people to feel pain.

Our apathy can cause people to be abused.

Of course, caring is costly; it can get you crucified. But the truth is there is only one thing more costly than caring, and that's not caring!

LEAVING THE WORLD A BETTER PLACE THAN YOU FOUND IT

Charles Kerault, on his famous "On the Road" program, talked one night to an elderly gentleman in Virginia. This older man had bought some land and had built a public park at his own expense. He put in picnic tables, recreational equipment, and all of the other things that make a public park. It was open to everyone.

Not only that, he also raised vegetables and tomatoes throughout the year and he would take these tomatoes and vegetables and put them on the picnic tables for anyone who wanted to come and eat them.

Charles Kerault asked him, "Why do you do all of this?" The man simply answered, "If you don't leave this world a better place than what you found it, what's the sense of your being here?"

Now, this elderly gentleman in the state of Virginia had discovered one of the keys to successful and meaningful living: to be able to see something that should be done and to take it on and do something about it.

When we stop and think about it, we see that the great people of faith in the Scriptures and down through the pages of history were those people who saw a situation that needed to be made better. They heard the call of God in that penetrating and personal question, "Why don't you correct this?" They had the courage to take up the torch, to speak the word, to do the deed, to face the challenge.

Let me show you what I mean.

First, I'm thinking of the story of Moses. He sits on a quiet, pastoral hillside, in Midian, but he is not at peace within. Inside, he is burning with concern for his people in Egyptian slavery. How can he know serenity of spirit when he knows the anguish of his people?

I imagine Moses thinking, "It's wrong! It's cruel. The Hebrew people are being overworked and underfed, misused and exploited by the Egyptian pharaoh. He is treating them worse than animals. It's unfair. It's unjust. Someone ought to do something about this terrible situation."

Then God appears to Moses in a burning bush and in essence he asks, "Why not you, Moses? Why don't you go and set my people free? Go, and I will go with you!"

You know the rest of the story. Moses takes up the torch, accepts the challenge, and leads the Hebrew people to freedom.

Second, I'm thinking of the story of Isaiah. He, too, is concerned. He lives in a time when his people have drifted away from the basics of their covenant faith. Their religion is shallow, their ethics are questionable, their business practices are shady. The poor are being exploited, people are being cheated, the nation is in danger of falling, and then to make matters worse, their King Uzziah dies.

Worried and downhearted, Isaiah goes to the temple to pray. There he experiences God. He realizes how bad the situation is. He sees that a prophet is needed for this hour (see Isaiah 6:1-8).

And then God's question explodes into his mind. "Why not you, Isaiah? Why don't you do something about this?"

You know what happens next. Isaiah hears the call and responds, "Here am I; send me!" (Isaiah 6:8).

Third, I'm thinking of the story of Jesus. He is having a successful ministry in Galilee, but he is bothered by what is happening in Jerusalem.

He sees how the people are being exploited in the temple. He sees how minute laws are getting in the way of love, kindness, and compassion. He sees religious hypocrisy and corruption. He knows that something should be done, someone should speak out, someone should strike a blow for justice.

He hears the call. He sees the need. And he sets his face toward Jerusalem. He cleanses the temple. He dies for what he believes. However, what he was and what he said and what he did and what he lived for cannot be killed, cannot be sealed in a tomb, cannot be silenced in a grave. It resurrected! He resurrected, and the torch he carried into Jerusalem still burns brightly.

THE CHRISTMAS GIFTS
THAT ALWAYS FIT

It was just a few days before Christmas and I was finally getting around to my Christmas shopping. Along with Santa, I was making a list and checking it twice, when I discovered that I needed another list, a list of sizes.

A "size list" is very important because we do want our gifts to fit. Also, over the years, I have noticed that sizes tend to change. (I'm referring to children's sizes here—not wives'!)

As I was working on my gift list, my mind drifted from the practical task at hand and I found myself thinking deeper thoughts about Christmas gifts that always fit and are always appropriate.

The Christmas gifts that always fit: What would they be? If you make a list like that, what would be on it? As you think about that—if you'll pardon the pun—let me ask you to try these on for size.

First, there is the gift of time: a Christmas gift that always fits. In the busy, hectic pace of Christmas, it may well be that the most precious and valuable gift we can give someone we love is a little slice of time, a little uninterrupted time just for them.

"The greatest gift I ever received," said a young, successful attorney, "was a gift I got one Christmas when my dad gave me a small box. Inside was a note that read, 'Son, this year I will give you 365 hours, an hour a day every day after dinner. It's yours! We'll talk about what you want to talk about, we'll go where you want to go, or play what you want to play. It will be your hour! This is my gift to you this year: the gift of time.'"

This raises an interesting question: Is there someone near you to whom you need to give a little time? College students home for the holidays and young people out of school for a few days who are wondering what they can do special for their parents during this sacred season may well discover that the best thing is to give them a little time. The gift of time is always appropriate. The gift of time always fits.

Second, there is the gift of kindness. This is the time when our emotions are taxed a bit and it is easy to become impatient and irritable. But it doesn't have to be that way. We don't have to be thoughtless or rude or edgy or harsh or hostile. We can be kind!

I think that one of the single most impressive emblems of Christian faith is kindness. You can be an authority in theology. You can speak of the great philosophers. You can master church history. You can quote verses of Scripture. But only when you show me kindness do I really begin to see your faith.

John Boyle O'Reilly expressed it powerfully in rhyme:

> "What is real Good?"
> I asked in musing mood.
>
> "Order," said the law court;
> "Knowledge," said the school;
> "Truth," said the wise man;
> "Pleasure," said the fool;
> "Love," said the maiden;
> "Beauty," said the page;
> "Freedom," said the dreamer;
> "Home," said the sage;
> "Fame," said the soldier;
> "Equity," said the seer.
> Spake my heart fully sad:
> "The answer is not here."

Then within my bosom,
Softly this I heard:
"Each heart holds the secret;
'Kindness' is the word!"

Is there someone near you who this Christmas needs, more than anything else, the gift of kindness?

Third, there is the gift of appreciation. We don't have to be thoughtless. We don't have to take people or things for granted. We can be appreciative and grateful. I am convinced that people are hungry for appreciation.

How long has it been since you told your parents or your children or your marriage partner or your neighbors or your coworkers how much you appreciate them? It may be the best gift you could give them. It's another gift that always fits.

Fourth, there is the gift of encouragement. There is a wonderful verse in the book of Isaiah where he says the Lord has given him the tongue that enables him to lift up the one who is weary (see Isaiah 50:4).

Wouldn't it be great if all of us had that ability to encourage people when they are tired, when they are down, when they are low? What could be a better gift than the gift of encouragement!

Fifth and finally, there is the most important gift that always fits and it is, of course, the gift of love. What the people near us need this season more than anything else is the gift of love.

As the hymn writer so aptly put it, "Love came down at Christmas." What could be more fitting than to receive that love and then to pass it on? As the poet put it:

> A bell is not a bell until it's rung,
> A song is not a song until it's sung.
> Love is not put into your heart to stay.
> Love is only love when you give it away!

Time, kindness, appreciation, encouragement, and love: these are a few Christmas gifts that always fit. I'm sure you will think of others. And, of course, these gifts are fitting gifts not only at Christmas. They are great gifts to give to everyone we meet all year round.

Discussion Guide
for James W. Moore's

THE POWER OF A STORY

John D. Schroeder

Finding God in Unexpected Places

1. Name some unexpected places where God appears.
2. Where do you normally expect to find God?
3. What can we learn from God's unexpected ways?
4. How are people changed after an unexpected appearance from God?

Are You Standing in God's Way?

1. Have you ever felt you were standing in God's way?
2. List some reasons we may hinder God's plans.
3. Name some little "gray sins." Why can they cause the most damage?
4. List ways our words and actions can affect others.

The Sin of Presumptuous Religion

1. Give an example of a presumptuous attitude.
2. What is the cure for presumptuousness?
3. Name some presumptions we need to avoid.
4. Why are people presumptuous? Name some causes.

Little Things Mean a Lot

1. Why is it often easy to be pulled apart by little things?
2. Name some little things that often bother us.
3. How should we cope with the little challenges of life?
4. Why are little resentments spiritual cancers?

The Power of Kindness

1. Recall a time you experienced the power of kindness.
2. Why does kindness have such power?
3. How are kindness and the Christian faith related?
4. Name some strategies for being a kinder person.

Have You Ever Been Reduced to a Shameful Silence?

1. Have you ever experienced or witnessed shameful silence? Explain.
2. What good can come from shameful silence?
3. How and why are people often like the quarreling disciples?
4. Give some examples of shameful situations.

The Amazing Serenity of Jesus

1. How was Jesus a model of serenity?
2. Contrast the differences between Jesus and Pilate.
3. How can we achieve inner peace and spiritual power?
4. What does serenity mean to you? Explain it in your own words.

Is There Any Hope?

1. Do you believe we are living in desperate times? Explain your response.
2. How do we maintain hope?
3. Why is hope necessary for a healthy life?
4. Where do you find hope?

Spiritual Maturity

1. In your own words, explain the meaning of spiritual maturity.
2. How do we achieve spiritual maturity?
3. Why are so many people spiritually immature?
4. Explain the connection between love and maturity.

Three Stages of Life

1. Name and define the three stages of life.
2. What does it mean to grow up?
3. Why is it dangerous to categorize others?
4. Name some acts of maturity.

Magnanimity—The Essential Spirit of the Christian

1. In your own words, explain the meaning of magnanimity.
2. Recall a time you witnessed magnanimity.
3. Why is the spirit of magnanimity an essential spirit of the Christian?
4. How can we be more magnanimous?

The Best Qualities in Life Are Reflections of God

1. List some of the best qualities in life.
2. Name some actions that reflect God.
3. What are some words that are reflections of God?
4. Name two qualities you admire most in a person.

The Healing Power of the Church

1. Explain what is meant by the healing power of the church.
2. List those in need of healing.
3. What is needed to experience healing?
4. Why does everyone need a support community?

Celebrating the Joy of the Journey

1. What is meant by the joy of the journey?
2. Name a time you experienced this joy.
3. How do we seize the joy of the journey?
4. Why do we need to learn the hard lessons of patience and trust?

The Dangers of the Blame Game

1. Name some situations where people play the blame game.
2. List some of the dangers of this game.
3. What role does taking responsibility play in solving this?
4. Suggest constructive alternatives to placing blame.

Five Different Ways to Learn the Truth

1. Why is it important to know the truth?
2. What often prevents people from finding the truth?
3. Which of the five ways do you prefer and why?
4. How do you distinguish the truth from a lie?

Agents of Forgiveness

1. Recall a time you experienced critical judgment.
2. How was Jesus a model for forgiveness?
3. Why are people and love top priorities?
4. What often prevents us from offering forgiveness?

Vicarious Lessons from the Foot of the Cross

1. Recall a lesson you learned vicariously.
2. List some dangers of being selfish.
3. What lessons do we learn from the words and actions of Judas and Pilate?
4. Name some of the lessons we learn from Jesus.

The Calling

1. List the ways that God calls us.
2. How do people react when called by God?
3. Compare and contrast Christian vocations with church-related vocations.
4. How can the church be more effective in helping people hear God's call?

Be Quick to Listen, Slow to Speak, and Slow to Anger

1. Why are we not always quick to listen?
2. Give some tips for being a better listener.
3. Why should most people talk a lot less?
4. When you get angry, what should you do?

Celebrating Your Own Uniqueness
and the Uniqueness of Others

1. Name something that makes you unique.
2. Why do people often want to force their way on to others?
3. What did Paul tell the Christians in Corinth?
4. How are love and uniqueness connected?

The Ahs and Blahs of Life

1. Share both an up and a down moment from your life.
2. How should we cope with blah moments?

3. What can we learn from the Apostle Paul about ups and downs?

4. List some times when life feels good.

Travel Light

1. Why do we need to travel light?
2. How do you distinguish between essential and excess baggage?
3. What three things should we take along and why?
4. List some tips for simplification.

The Power of Love

1. In your own words, define the power of love.
2. Share a time you experienced love's power.
3. What choices do we face in hard times?
4. List ways to rise above problems.

God Is with Us . . . Always

1. What lessons can we learn from the John Todd story?
2. Why do we fear death?
3. Why can we trust God's promises?
4. How do you know God is with you?

We Are God's Family

1. Why do we need repeated reminders from God and the Bible?
2. How are we to treat other family members?
3. What do God's commandments tell us?
4. How is God's family different from other families?

We Have Met the Enemy and He Is Us

1. Why are we often our own worst enemy?
2. Name some common "troubles within" we all face.
3. How does faith release us from faceless fears?
4. What should you do with your fears?

Use It or Lose It

1. Share your thoughts on the wisdom of Matthew 25:29.
2. List some ways our talents are wasted.
3. Why is this principle true on so many levels?
4. How have you lived this principle?

Why Do We Wait for Permission?

1. What lessons can we learn from the encounter of Jesus and the woman in the synagogue?
2. List some reasons people wait for permission to live.
3. Why don't we need permission?
4. Define what it means to really live.

Not Trying Is Worse Than Trying and Failing

1. Name some times people are tempted to quit on life.
2. Explain the danger of not trying.
3. Recall a time you tried and failed.
4. Recall a time you tried and succeeded.

Success, Failure: How Do You Tell the Difference?

1. How would you define success and failure?
2. Why do people often equate success with wealth?
3. What does Jesus teach us about success?
4. List some ways to be a servant.

Turning Problems into Opportunities

1. Why can't we outrun our problems?
2. How did Jesus show us how to cope with problems?
3. Share a time you coped with a problem.
4. How can God help us with our problems?

Clowns and Prophets

1. Why are clowns and prophets not taken seriously?
2. Name some advice given to us by prophets.
3. Why do we continue to have wars?
4. How has war affected your life?

The Battle Within

1. Name some destructive attitudes within us.
2. What attitude is your worst enemy?
3. Why is our inner life so important?
4. How can God help us win our inner battles?

Jesus Gives God a Face

1. What does the Gospel of Luke tell us about God?
2. Explain why we see God in Jesus.
3. Compare and contrast life before and after Jesus.
4. When you think of God, what comes to mind?

What Is the Subtle Difference?

1. Why do people experience subtle differences?
2. What role does response play?
3. What is the difference between responding and reacting?
4. Explain the meaning of conversion.

Dealing with Disappointment Creatively

1. List some common disappointments in life.
2. Recall a time you were disappointed.
3. Name the seven suggested strategies and tell which ones help you the most.
4. What will you do the next time you encounter disappointment?

Three Breakthroughs That Can Change Your Life

1. Why are many people imprisoned by ruts?
2. Tell why you do not have to be a victim of your circumstances.
3. How can you escape from being a victim of pride?
4. Explain why death is not to be feared.

Are You Eager to Be Apathetic?

1. Why is apathy a big problem?
2. What is the cause of apathy?
3. How can we overcome apathy?
4. Name some acts of caring.

Leaving the World a Better Place Than You Found It

1. What lessons can we learn from the life of Moses?
2. How and why did Isaiah respond to a bad situation?
3. What lessons can we learn from Jesus about taking action?
4. List simple things anyone can do to make the world a better place.

The Christmas Gifts That Always Fit

1. What is the best Christmas gift you ever received?
2. How can we give the gift of time?
3. Why are kindness and appreciation good gifts?
4. How can you give love and encouragement?